On a Roll Again!

14 CREATIVE QUILTS FROM JELLY ROLL STRIPS

COMPILED BY **LISSA ALEXANDER**

Martingale®
Create with Confidence

Moda All-Stars
On a Roll Again! 14 Creative Quilts from Jelly Roll Strips
© 2021 by Martingale & Company®

Martingale®
18939 120th Ave. NE, Ste. 101
Bothell, WA 98011-9511 USA
ShopMartingale.com

Printed in Hong Kong
26 25 24 23 22 21   8 7 6 5 4 3 2 1

Library of Congress Cataloging-in-Publication Data is available upon request.

ISBN: 978-1-68356-135-4

MISSION STATEMENT

We empower makers who use fabric and yarn to make life more enjoyable.

CREDITS

PUBLISHER AND CHIEF VISIONARY OFFICER
Jennifer Erbe Keltner

CONTENT DIRECTOR
Karen Costello Soltys

DESIGN MANAGER
Adrienne Smitke

TECHNICAL EDITOR
Nancy Mahoney

PRODUCTION MANAGER
Regina Girard

COPY EDITOR
Sheila Chapman Ryan

PHOTOGRAPHERS
Adam Albright
Brent Kane

ILLUSTRATOR
Sandy Loi

Contents

Introduction

Truly, I couldn't be happier with the fantastic batch of quilts the Moda All-Stars designers have created just for you. Each quilt starts with a Jelly Roll, but I think you'll agree, the designs are so clever that it's hard to tell they begin with 2½"-wide precut strips. From simply stunning to downright charming, the projects are fabulous. You may have a difficult time deciding which one to make first!

At Moda Fabrics, we're always ready to roll, especially when it comes to making quilts from Jelly Rolls! What makes 2½"-wide strip quilt patterns so popular? With much of the cutting work done for you, you'll quickly get to the fun part—sitting at your sewing machine!

As with all Moda All-Stars books, we're happy to donate the royalties from this book to a worthy organization. This time we've chosen World Central Kitchen (wck.org). This organization's mission is to feed those in need—which is more important now than ever, as I write this in the midst of a global pandemic. As of late 2020, World Central Kitchen has served over 33 million meals in more than 400 cities.

By purchasing this book, not only can you look forward to fun times sewing, but you can feel good that funds from your purchase are going to help families in need. We thank you from the bottom of our hearts.

Now let's get rolling. Grab your favorite Jelly Rolls and let's sew!

~ Lissa Alexander

Sewing with Jelly Rolls

If you're new to sewing with Jelly Rolls, or if you've used them before but wondered about how to handle the pinked edges, control the lint, or where to sew for a perfect ¼" seam allowance, you'll want to read this section. Moda Jelly Rolls are precut strips of fabric that measure 2½" × the width of fabric. You get 40 strips in each Jelly Roll. And, they generally come shrink-wrapped in plastic. This is so they don't become frayed or dirty during handling in shipping and while on display at your favorite quilt shop. After you tear off the plastic, you'll notice the edges are shallowly pinked and that there is a bit of lint along the edges. What to do about all of that?

DEALING WITH THE LINT

Moda All-Star Corey Yoder (her Pretty Frames quilt pattern is on page 31) recommends using a lint roller on each side of the Jelly Roll before unrolling the strips to remove as much of the lint as possible before you get started. Easy!

Swipe a lint roller over each side of the Jelly Roll several times to remove the bulk of the lint.

If you prefer to use starch on your fabrics when sewing, Moda fabric designer Laurie Simpson shares that she empties a bottle of liquid starch into a pail and then squishes the unrolled strips in the pail to saturate them. Remove a couple of strips at a time, squeeze out the excess starch, and then hang them on a drying rack. Press them flat when the starch has dried and you're good to go.

Another Moda fabric designer, Betsy Chutchian, delints her fabric rolls by placing them in the dryer. She doesn't unroll them first, but turns the dryer on high heat and runs it for six to eight minutes. Then she cleans out the lint trap and repeats. She insists that the strips don't become tangled and they come out smooth and unwrinkled. And all the lint collects in the dryer's lint trap. But don't forget to clean it out!

DEALING WITH THE PINKED EDGES

One question that is frequently asked about sewing with strips that have pinked edges is "Where do I line up the fabric to get a ¼" seam allowance?" We have a couple of tips to help you here. Whichever you choose, be sure to sew with a scant ¼" seam allowance. By scant, we mean sew one or two thread widths narrower than a full ¼".

OPTION 1: Trim the strips first. If the pinked edges bother you, you can trim a very narrow bit off the edges of your strips. However, you'll need to make an adjustment when sewing to sew a very scant ¼" seam allowance. Why? Because you'll need to account for the amount you've trimmed off and you don't want your strip-pieced project to turn out too small. It's best to trim and then test your seam allowance to make sure the pieces turn out the correct size.

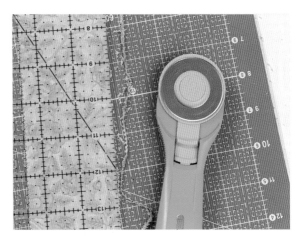

Trim off the bulk of the pinked edges, but don't trim away too much or you won't have enough width left for patterns that call for 2½"-wide pieces.

After trimming the pinked edges, sew with a "very scant" ¼" seam allowance.

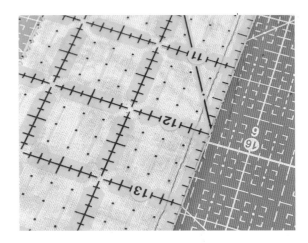

Notice how narrow the seam allowance is? That's because the pinked edges have already been trimmed away.

OPTION 2: Measure the strips to decide where to sew. What do we mean by that? Measure the width of a sample strip to see if it's 2½" wide from the outer point of the pinked edge or from the inner points. The reason you want to measure is that it makes a difference if you've dried your strips in a dryer or starched them—or if you're using them straight from the Jelly Roll. They may have shrunk slightly from the dryer heat or the heat of the iron after starching. But generally, they will shrink in length, not in width. Measuring helps you determine where you need to sew—whether that's aligning the outer points with your seam guide or the inner points or somewhere between the two.

Once you decide where to sew, stitch a scant ¼" seam allowance. Before pressing the strips open, use your ruler to measure 2" from the seamline. If you have excess pinked edges extending beyond the edge of a ruler, trim them off with your rotary cutter. Then you can proceed to subcut units and continue sewing with a scant ¼" seam allowance throughout your project.

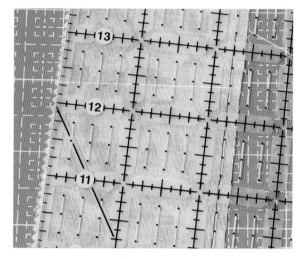

After sewing a scant ¼" seam allowance, measure 2¼" from the stitched seamline. If you have any pinked edges extending beyond the ruler, you can trim them off.

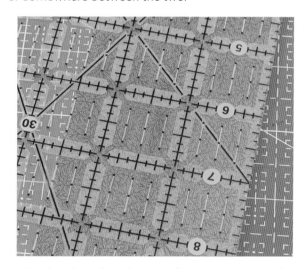

Notice that the Jelly Roll strip is 2½" wide, measuring from the outer points on each side of the strip.

Favorite Tools for Sewing with Jelly Rolls

We asked your favorite Moda designers which tool or gadget they wouldn't be without when it comes to sewing with Jelly Rolls. Can you guess who offered each of the answers below? (To learn the answers, you'll need to read each of the "Rollin' with..." sidebars.)

MODA ALL-STARS

Susan Ache

Sandy Klop

Lisa Bongean

Janet Clare

Joanna Figueroa

Corey Yoder

Barbara Groves

Lynne Hagmeier

Lissa Alexander

Sherri McConnell

April Rosenthal

Anne Sutton

Vanessa Goertzen

Vanessa Christenson

FAVORITE TOOLS AND GADGETS

Favorite pins

Steam iron and wool pressing mat

Pajama pants

Wool pincushion

Seam ripper

Bloc Loc rulers

My Bernina

A clean work surface

Diagonal seam tape

Spray starch (more than one All-Star agrees!)

M&Ms

Good lighting

Old metal sewing machine

9

Check the Box

Once you've added this beauty to your must-make list, you'll be ready to check all the boxes—fun to make, easier than it looks, and a certified fabulous finish that your friends and family will admire!

FINISHED QUILT: 69½" × 69½" | FINISHED BLOCK: 10" × 10"

MATERIALS

Yardage is based on 42"-wide fabric; Jelly Rolls contain 40 strips, 2½" × width of fabric. Susan used Mackinac Island by Minick and Simpson.

- 1 Jelly Roll of assorted light, medium, and dark prints for blocks
- 1⅞ yards of white solid for blocks, sashing, and inner border
- ½ yard of pink print for middle border
- 2⅛ yards of blue floral for outer border and binding
- 4¼ yards of fabric for backing
- 76" × 76" piece of batting
- Template plastic or Companion Angle ruler by Darlene Zimmerman

CUTTING

All measurements include ¼" seam allowances.

From *each* of 26 assorted medium and dark strips, cut:
1 A strip, 2¼" × 42" (26 total)

From *each* of 7 assorted light strips, cut:
2 B strips, 1¼" × 42" (14 total; 1 is extra)

From *1* of the assorted light strips, cut:
25 squares, 1½" × 1½"

From the white solid, cut:
39 strips, 1½" × 42"; crosscut *33 of the strips* into:
    16 strips, 1½" × 11½"
    24 strips, 1½" × 10½"
    100 strips, 1½" × 7½"

From the pink print, cut:
6 strips, 2" × 42"

From the *lengthwise* grain of the blue floral, cut:
2 strips, 5½" × 69½"
2 strips, 5½" × 59½"
5 strips, 2½" × 58"

MAKING THE BLOCKS

Press seam allowances in the directions indicated by the arrows.

1 If you're not using the Companion Angle ruler, you'll need to make a triangle-cutting template. To make a template, trace the triangle pattern on page 16 onto template plastic. Use utility scissors to cut out the template *exactly* on the drawn lines.

2 Staggering the ends by 1", join two different print A strips and one B strip to make a strip set measuring 4¾" × 42", including seam allowances. Make 13 strip sets.

Make 13 strip sets.

3 Align the top blunted edge of the triangle template or ruler with the top edge of the strip set. Cut along both angled sides of the template to make a triangle. Rotate the template or ruler and align the angled edge with the newly cut edge and the blunted tip with the bottom edge of the strip set. Cut along the right edge of the template to make a triangle. Cut eight triangles from each strip set (104 total), keeping like units together. You'll have four units left over.

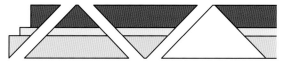

Cut 8 triangles from each strip set
(104 total).

4 Lay out four matching units from step 3, four white 1½" × 7½" strips, and one light 1½" square, noting the orientation of the units. Join the pieces into rows, and then sew the rows together. Make 25 blocks.

Make 25 blocks.

5 Trim the ends of the white strips even with the edges of the side triangles. The blocks should measure 10½" square, including seam allowances.

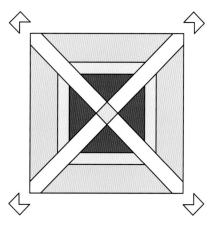

Trim corners of each block.

Designed and pieced by Susan Ache; quilted by Susan Rogers

ASSEMBLING THE QUILT TOP

Refer to the quilt assembly diagram below as needed throughout.

1 Join five blocks and four white 1½" × 10½" strips to make a block row. Make five rows measuring 10½" × 54½", including seam allowances.

2 Join four white 1½" × 11½" strips and one white 1½" × 10½" strip to make a sashing row. Make four rows measuring 1½" × 54½", including seam allowances.

3 Join the block rows alternately with the sashing rows, aligning the seam intersections of the blocks and sashing with those in the sashing rows. The quilt-top center should measure 54½" square, including seam allowances.

4 Join the remaining white 1½"-wide strips end to end. From the pieced strip, cut two 54½"-long strips and two 56½"-long strips. Sew the shorter strips to opposite sides of the quilt center. Sew the longer strips to the top and bottom edges. The quilt top should measure 56½" square, including seam allowances.

5 Join the pink 2"-wide strips end to end. From the pieced strip, cut two 56½"-long strips and two 59½"-long strips. Sew the shorter strips to opposite sides of the quilt top. Sew the longer strips to the top and bottom edges. The quilt top should measure 59½" square, including seam allowances.

6 Sew the blue 59½"-long strips to opposite sides of the quilt top. Sew the blue 69½"-long strips to the top and bottom edges. The quilt top should measure 69½" square.

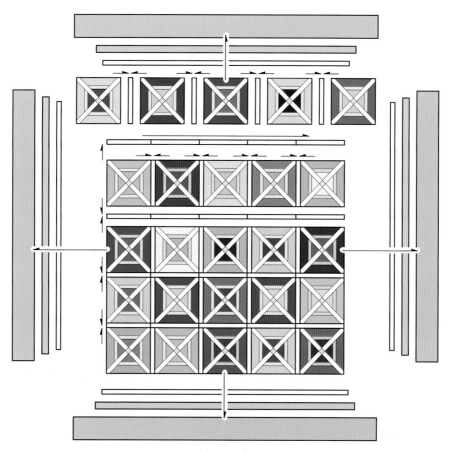

Quilt assembly

FINISHING THE QUILT

For more details on any finishing steps, visit ShopMartingale.com/HowtoQuilt for free downloadable information.

1 Layer the quilt top with batting and backing; baste the layers together.

2 Quilt by hand or machine. Susan's quilt is machine quilted with an allover design of circles, stars, and swirls.

3 Use the blue 2½"-wide strips to make binding and then attach the binding to the quilt.

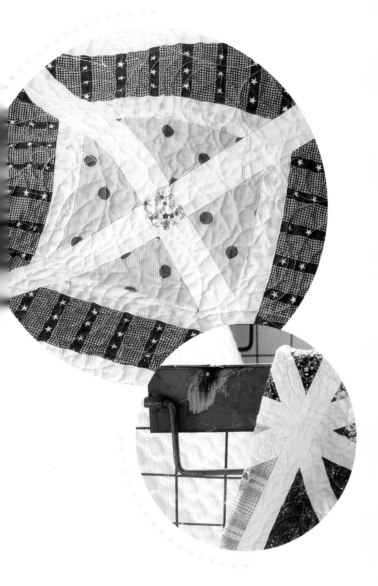

ROLLIN' WITH
Susan Ache

@yardgrl60 on Instagram

I'd like to give a round of applause to quilters who alter any quilt pattern to make it their own.

To start the ball rolling on a new project, I make sure my sewing space is all clear and cleaned up before the new tornado blows through!

Two phrases that roll off the tongue easily at my house are "Hurry up" and "Are you ready yet?" (each phrase said as one long and loud word).

I'd gladly roll out the welcome mat for a guest from the past, Ernest Hemingway, and of course a guest from the present, Ina Garten, who is more than welcome to work in my kitchen with me.

To round out my sewing basics of a ruler, mat, rotary cutter, and scissors, I'd add more Bloc Loc rulers.

I'd roll out the red carpet for the person who invented the Dewey decimal system, Melvil Dewey.

When I let the good times roll, I'm sure to have strawberry licorice in a suitcase while traveling, Ruffles potato chips at home, and my phone and a diet Dr Pepper always. But above all, the good times won't roll unless my hair is clean!

I just roll with it when nothing is going according to schedule.

My cats **have me wrapped around their little paws.**

When I'm making the rounds at local quilt shops, I make sure to check out all of the bundles first, hunt for my favorite fabrics to buy more, and check out the class samples hanging on the wall.

Ask around and my friends will tell you I'm . . . hmm, can I phone a friend to ask?

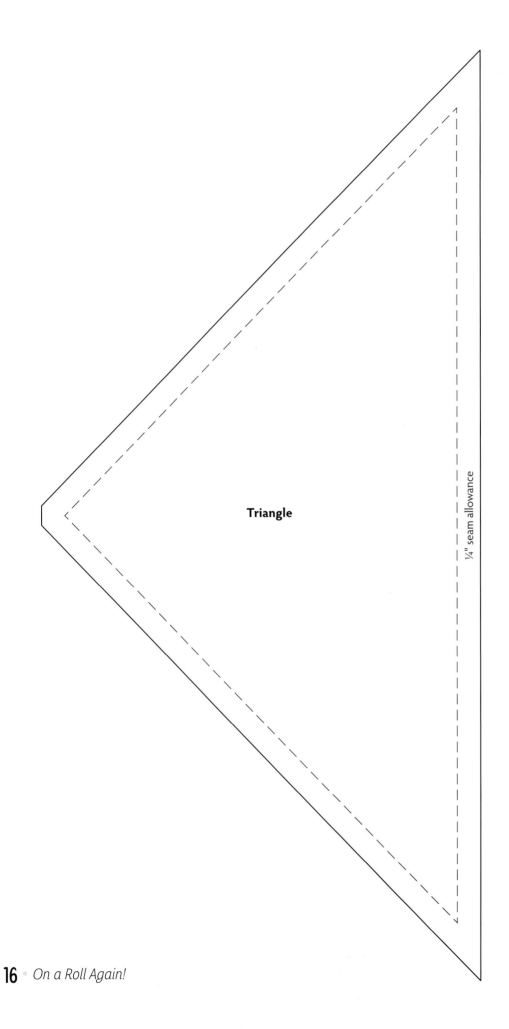

Triangle

¼" seam allowance

Boogie

Boogie, a catchy and repetitive blues-based rhythm, inspired this quick and simply pieced quilt using Janet Clare's fabric collection called The Blues. These fabrics were influenced by the Jazz Age, blues music, The Great Gatsby by F. Scott Fitzgerald, and Josephine Baker's pet cheetah.

FINISHED QUILT: 66½" × 66½" | FINISHED BLOCK: 22" × 22"

MATERIALS

Yardage is based on 42"-wide fabric; Jelly Rolls contain 40 strips, 2½" × width of fabric. Janet used The Blues by Janet Clare.

- 3 Jelly Rolls of assorted blue and cream prints for blocks and binding
- 4⅛ yards of fabric for backing
- 73" × 73" piece of batting

Fabric Combinations

Before you start cutting, separate the Jelly Roll strips into nine groups of nine strips each and label the strips A–D as listed below. Refer to the photo on page 20 and the block diagram on page 19 for placement guidance. Use the A and B strips for the interior parts of the block, the C strips for the outer edges, and the D strips for the block sashing. Notice that the pieces on the outside edges are light in some blocks and dark in other blocks.

- **A:** two matching strips
- **B:** two matching strips
- **C:** three matching strips
- **D:** two matching strips

CUTTING

Before cutting, separate your strips into groups as indicated in "Fabric Combinations" on page 17. Repeat these cutting instructions to make nine blocks, keeping the pieces for each block together. All measurements include ¼" seam allowances.

Cutting for 1 Block

From 2 A strips, cut a *total* of:
2 rectangles, 2½" × 10½"
2 rectangles, 2½" × 8½"
2 rectangles, 2½" × 6½"
2 rectangles, 2½" × 4½"
2 squares, 2½" × 2½"

From 2 B strips, cut a *total* of:
2 rectangles, 2½" × 10½"
2 rectangles, 2½" × 8½"
2 rectangles, 2½" × 6½"
2 rectangles, 2½" × 4½"
2 squares, 2½" × 2½"

From 3 C strips, cut a *total* of:
4 rectangles, 2½" × 8½"
4 rectangles, 2½" × 6½"
4 rectangles, 2½" × 4½"
4 squares, 2½" × 2½"

From 2 D strips, cut a *total* of:
4 rectangles, 2½" × 10½"

Cutting for Block Centers

From the remaining A, B, and C strips, cut a *total* of:
9 squares, 2½" × 2½" (E)

MAKING THE BLOCKS

For each block use one group of A–D pieces and one contrasting E square. Press seam allowances in the directions indicated by the arrows.

1 Lay out one of each A piece and one of each C piece in five columns as shown. Sew the pieces into columns and then join the columns to make a quarter-block unit. Make two matching units measuring 10½" square, including seam allowances.

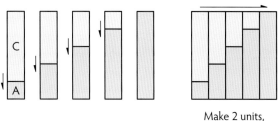

Make 2 units,
10½" × 10½".

2 Lay out one of each B piece and one of each C piece in five columns as shown. Sew the pieces into columns and then join the columns to make a quarter-block unit. Make two matching units measuring 10½" square, including seam allowances.

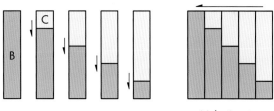

Make 2 units,
10½" × 10½".

3 Lay out the quarter-block units from steps 1 and 2, four matching D rectangles, and one contrasting E square. Sew the pieces into rows. Join the rows to make a block. Repeat the steps to make nine blocks measuring 22½" square, including seam allowances.

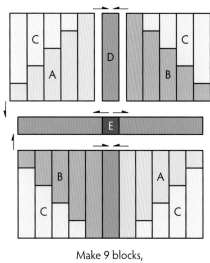

Make 9 blocks,
22½" × 22½".

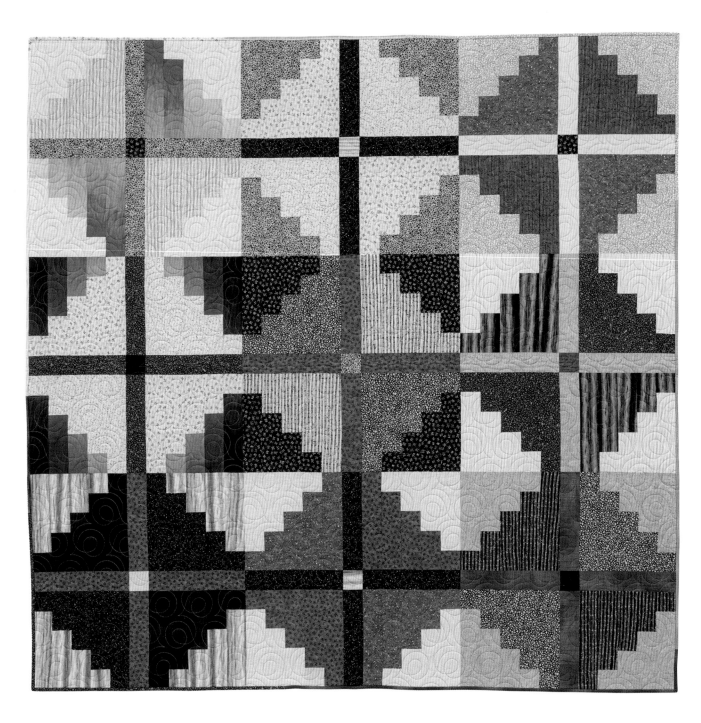

Designed and pieced by Janet Clare; quilted by Carolyn Clark

ASSEMBLING THE QUILT TOP

Lay out the blocks in three rows of three blocks each as shown in the quilt assembly diagram. Sew the blocks into rows and then join the rows. The quilt top should measure 66½" square.

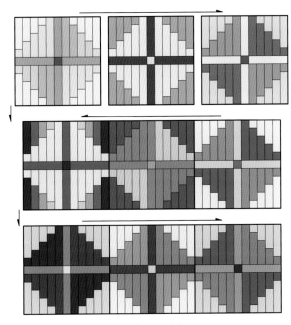

Quilt assembly

FINISHING THE QUILT

For more details on any finishing steps, visit ShopMartingale.com/HowtoQuilt for free downloadable information.

1. Layer the quilt top with batting and backing; baste the layers together.

2. Quilt by hand or machine. Janet's quilt is machine quilted with an allover motif of loops and swirls.

3. Use seven of the remaining blue 2½"-wide strips to make binding and then attach the binding to the quilt.

ROLLIN' WITH
Janet Clare

JanetClare.co.uk

I'd like to give a round of applause to quilters who finish *all* of their projects.

To start the ball rolling on a new project, I put the iron on.

One phrase that rolls off the tongue easily at my house is "Put the kettle on."

I'd roll out the red carpet for the person who invented spray starch.

I roll into my sewing room around 11:00 a.m., "elevenses."

When I let the good times roll, I'm sure to have a gin and tonic!

I just roll with it when everything goes wonky.

My dog Betty **has me wrapped around her little paw.**

When I'm making the rounds at local quilt shops, I make sure to introduce myself.

In my home, we tend to gather 'round the kitchen table.

Ask around and my friends will tell you I'm hard to get a hold of. Sorry, friends!

Stacked Stars

If fall had a flag, this might well be its design! With an autumnal rainbow of Mother Nature's richest hues cascading across a cozy throw, you'll be ready to wrap up in this stunner before the first leaves flutter down from the trees.

FINISHED QUILT: 66½" × 72½"

MATERIALS

Yardage is based on 42"-wide fabric; Jelly Rolls contain 40 strips, 2½" × width of fabric. Lynne used Bittersweet Lane by Kansas Troubles Quilters.

- 1 Jelly Roll of assorted tan prints for squares and rectangles
- 1 Jelly Roll of assorted gold, pumpkin, red, purple, blue, green, and brown prints for squares and rectangles*
- ½ yard of tan print for inner border
- 2 yards of green print for outer border and binding
- 4½ yards of fabric for backing
- 73" × 79" piece of batting

*To achieve the look of the quilt shown on page 28, you'll need at least 4 strips of each color. The fabrics do not need to be the same print, just the same color, such as navy, brown, or gold.

CUTTING

As you cut, label the pieces and keep like fabrics together. The letter labels refer to where the pieces will be used in the layout, which you can see on pages 26 and 27. All measurements include ¼" seam allowances.

From *each of 5* tan strips, cut:
6 rectangles, 2½" × 4½" (B; 30 total)
1 square, 2½" × 2½" (A; 5 total)

From *each of 7* tan strips, cut:
1 rectangle, 2½" × 6½" (C; 7 total)
4 rectangles, 2½" × 4½" (B; 28 total)
2 squares, 2½" × 2½" (A; 14 total)

From *each of 7* tan strips, cut:
1 rectangle, 2½" × 6½" (C; 7 total)
3 rectangles, 2½" × 4½" (B; 21 total)
2 squares, 2½" × 2½" (A; 14 total)

From *each of 3* tan strips, cut:
1 rectangle, 2½" × 8½" (D; 3 total)
3 rectangles, 2½" × 4½" (B; 9 total)
1 square, 2½" × 2½" (A; 3 total)

From *each of 4* tan strips, cut:
5 rectangles, 2½" × 4½" (B; 20 total)
1 square, 2½" × 2½" (A; 4 total)

From *each of 2* tan strips, cut:
1 rectangle, 2½" × 8½" (D; 2 total)
4 rectangles, 2½" × 4½" (B; 8 total)
1 square, 2½" × 2½" (A; 2 total)

From *each of 2* gold, pumpkin, red, purple, blue, green, and brown strips, cut:
4 rectangles, 2½" × 6½" (G; 56 total)
2 squares, 2½" × 2½" (E; 28 total)

Continued on page 24

Continued from page 23

From *each of 2* gold, pumpkin, red, purple, blue, green, and brown strips, cut:

4 rectangles, 2½" × 6½" (G; 56 total)

1 rectangle, 2½" × 4½" (F; 14 total)

2 squares, 2½" × 2½" (E; 28 total)

From the tan print for inner border, cut:

6 strips, 2½" × 42"

From the *lengthwise* grain of the green print for outer border, cut:

2 strips, 6½" × 66½"

2 strips, 6½" × 60½"

5 strips, 2½" × 60"

MAKING THE UNITS

Before you begin sewing, pair the pieces from one dark strip with the pieces from one tan strip. Refer to the photo on page 28 and the diagrams on pages 26 and 27 as needed throughout. After making the units, return each unit to its correct place in the quilt layout for each color section. Press seam allowances in the directions indicated by the arrows.

1 On a design wall, lay out the E squares and B rectangles for flying-geese units; the A and E squares for half-square-triangle units; the E squares and B, C, and D rectangles for single star-point units; the F and G rectangles; and the remaining A squares, B rectangles, and C rectangles in seven color sections. You should have four rows in each color section. The pieces in each row should consist of one tan and one dark. The pieces in each section should form a star on the left end of the section.

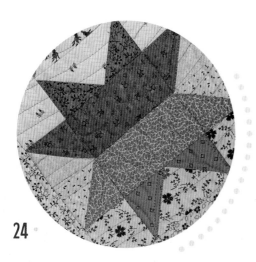

2 To make half-square-triangle units, draw a diagonal line from corner to corner on the wrong side of a tan A square. Layer a marked square on a gold E square, right sides together. Sew on the marked line. Trim the excess corner fabric ¼" from the stitched line to make a unit measuring 2½" square, including seam allowances. Repeat to make the number of units indicated of each color.

Make 2 gold units, 2½" × 2½".

Make 3 pumpkin units,   Make 2 red units, 2½" × 2½".   2½" × 2½".

Make 2 purple units,   Make 3 blue units, 2½" × 2½".   2½" × 2½".

Make 2 green units,   Make 2 brown units, 2½" × 2½".   2½" × 2½".

3 To make the flying-geese units, draw a line from corner to corner on the wrong side of four gold E squares. Place a marked square on one end of a tan B rectangle, right sides together. Sew on the marked line. Trim the corner fabric ¼" from the stitched line. Place an E square on the opposite end of the B rectangle. Sew and trim to make a unit measuring 2½" × 4½", including seam allowances. Make two gold units.

Make 2 gold units, 2½" × 4½".

4 Using the pumpkin, red, purple, blue, green, and brown E squares instead of gold ones, repeat step 3 to make two flying-geese units from each color.

Make 2 pumpkin units, 2½" × 4½".

Make 2 red units, 2½" × 4½".

Make 2 purple units, 2½" × 4½".

Make 2 blue units, 2½" × 4½".

Make 2 green units, 2½" × 4½".

Make 2 brown units, 2½" × 4½".

5 To make a single star-point C unit, draw a diagonal line from corner to corner on the wrong side of a gold E square. Place a marked square on one end of a tan C rectangle, right sides together. Sew on the marked line. Trim the excess corner fabric ¼" from the stitched line to make a gold unit measuring 2½" × 6½", including seam allowances. Repeat to make one red, one purple, one green, and one brown unit.

Make 1 gold, 1 red, 1 purple, 1 green, and 1 brown unit, 2½" × 6½".

6 To make a single star-point D unit, draw a diagonal line from corner to corner on the wrong side of a gold E square. Place a marked square on one end of a tan D rectangle, right sides together. Sew on the marked line. Trim the excess corner fabric ¼" from the stitched line to make a gold unit

Lynne Boster Hagmeier

KTQuilts.com

I'd like to give a round of applause to quilters who try something new.

To start the ball rolling on a new project, I tidy up my sewing space.

I'd gladly roll out the welcome mat for George Clooney.

To round out my sewing basics of a ruler, mat, rotary cutter, and scissors, I'd add good lighting.

I'd roll out the red carpet for the person who invented Twizzlers.

When I let the good times roll, I'm sure to have a little Skinnygirl vodka in my black raspberry Sparkling Ice.

I just roll with it when a block isn't perfect.

My grandkids have me wrapped around their little fingers.

When I'm making the rounds at local quilt shops, I make sure to add to my Moda mini charm collection.

In my home, we tend to gather 'round the fire pit.

Ask around and my friends will tell you I'm addicted to antiques.

measuring 2½" × 8½", including seam allowances. Repeat to make one purple and one brown unit.

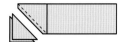

Make 1 gold, 1 purple, and 1 brown unit, 2½" × 8½".

7 To make a single star-point B unit, draw a diagonal line from corner to corner on the wrong side of a pumpkin E square. Place a marked square on one end of a tan B rectangle, right sides together. Sew on the marked line. Trim the excess corner fabric ¼" from the stitched line to make a pumpkin unit measuring 2½" × 4½", including seam allowances. Repeat to make one red, one blue, and one green unit.

Make 1 pumpkin, 1 red, 1 blue, and 1 green unit, 2½" × 4½".

ASSEMBLING THE QUILT TOP

1 For the gold section, join the squares, units, and rectangles into rows as shown. Join the rows to make a gold section measuring 8½" × 50½", including seam allowances. Repeat to make one purple and one brown section.

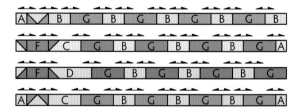

Make 1 gold section, 1 purple section, and 1 brown section, 8½" × 50½".

2 For the pumpkin section, join the squares, units, and rectangles into rows as shown. Join the rows to make a pumpkin section measuring 8½" × 50½", including seam allowances. Repeat to make a blue section.

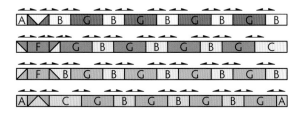

Make 1 pumpkin section and 1 blue section, 8½" × 50½".

3 For the red section, join the squares, units, and rectangles into rows as shown. Join the rows to make a red section measuring 8½" × 50½", including seam allowances. Repeat to make a green section.

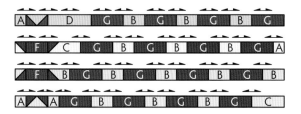

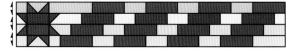

Make 1 red section and 1 green section, 8½" × 50½".

4 Join the sections to make a quilt-top center measuring 50½" × 56½", including seam allowances.

Quilt assembly

Designed and pieced by Lynne Boster Hagmeier; quilted by Joy Johnson

ADDING THE BORDERS

Press all seam allowances toward each newly added border.

1 For the inner border, join the tan 2½"-wide strips end to end. From the pieced strip, cut two 56½"-long strips and two 54½"-long strips. Sew the longer strips to opposite sides of the quilt center. Sew the shorter strips to the top and bottom edges. The quilt top should measure 54½" × 60½", including seam allowances.

2 For the outer border, sew the green 60½"-long strips to opposite sides of the quilt center. Sew the green 66½"-long strips to the top and bottom edges. The quilt top should measure 66½" × 72½".

FINISHING THE QUILT

For more details on any finishing steps, visit ShopMartingale.com/HowtoQuilt for free downloadable information.

1 Layer the quilt top with batting and backing; baste the layers together.

2 Quilt by hand or machine. Lynne's quilt is machine quilted with horizontal wavy lines in the quilt center and an ogee design in the outer border.

3 Use the green 2½"-wide strips to make binding and then attach the binding to the quilt.

Pretty Frames

If you've had your eye on a specialty print that's just too perfect to slice into small pieces, give it center stage here as block centers, then surround it with supporting strips from a coordinating Jelly Roll.

FINISHED QUILT: 64½" × 77½" | **FINISHED BLOCK: 12" × 12"**

MATERIALS

Yardage is based on 42"-wide fabric; Jelly Rolls contain 40 strips, 2½" × width of fabric. Corey used Spring Brook by Corey Yoder.

- 1 Jelly Roll of assorted prints for blocks
- 1⅓ yards of gray floral for blocks
- 2⅞ yards of white solid for blocks and sashing
- ⅜ yard of blue floral for sashing
- ⅝ yard of multicolored diagonal stripe for binding
- 4¾ yards of fabric for backing
- 71" × 84" piece of batting

CUTTING

All measurements include ¼" seam allowances.

From 35 assorted print strips, cut a *total* of:
240 rectangles, 2½" × 5¼"

From the gray floral, cut:
6 strips, 7" × 42"; crosscut into 30 squares, 7" × 7"

From the white solid, cut:
41 strips, 1½" × 42"; crosscut into:
　　60 strips, 1½" × 9"
　　60 strips, 1½" × 7"
　　49 strips, 1½" × 8½"
　　20 squares, 1½" × 1½"
7 strips, 4¼" × 42"; crosscut into 60 squares,
　　4¼" × 4¼". Cut the squares in half diagonally
　　to yield 120 triangles.

From the blue floral, cut:
7 strips, 1½" × 42"; crosscut into 98 rectangles,
　　1½" × 2½"

From the multicolored diagonal stripe, cut:
8 strips, 2½" × 42"

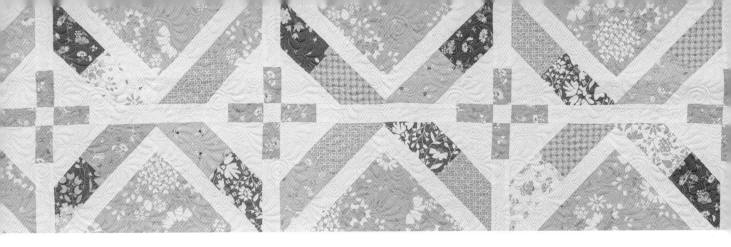

MAKING THE BLOCKS

Press seam allowances in the directions indicated by the arrows.

1 Sew white 1½" × 7" strips to opposite sides of a gray floral square. Sew white 1½" × 9" strips to the top and bottom edges to make a center unit. Make 30 units measuring 9" square, including seam allowances.

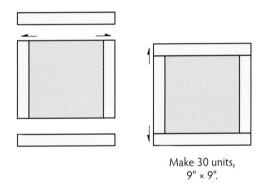

Make 30 units,
9" × 9".

2 Join two of the assorted print rectangles to make a side unit. Make 120 units measuring 2½" × 10", including seam allowances.

Make 120 units,
2½" × 10".

3 Center and sew side units to opposite sides of a center unit. Note that the side units will extend beyond the edges of the center unit; excess fabric will be trimmed later. Center and sew side units to the top and bottom edges of the center unit. Make 30 units measuring 13" square, including seam allowances.

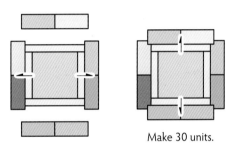

Make 30 units.

4 Fold four white triangles in half and lightly crease to mark the center of the long side. Sew the triangles to the unit from step 3, matching the center crease to the seamline. Repeat to make 30 blocks.

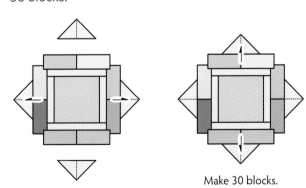

Make 30 blocks.

5 Trim and square up the blocks to measure 12½" square, making sure to keep the gray floral square centered.

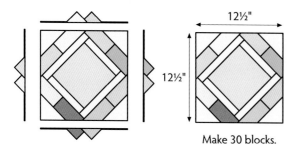

Make 30 blocks.

Easy Does It

If you own a 12½" square ruler, use it to easily center and square up the blocks. If you don't already have one, consider investing in one. It's so helpful not only for this block but for squaring up blocks in other projects or for cutting any squares 12½" or smaller. Most ruler brands offer a 12½" square, so choose your favorite and make quick work of trimming!

ASSEMBLING THE QUILT TOP

Refer to the quilt assembly diagram on page 35 as needed throughout.

1 Sew blue rectangles to both ends of a white 1½" × 8½" strip to make a sashing strip. Make 49 sashing strips measuring 1½" × 12½", including seam allowances.

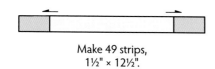

Make 49 strips,
1½" × 12½".

I'd like to give a round of applause to quilters who manage to label all of their quilts!

To start the ball rolling on a new project, I choose fabrics.

One phrase that rolls off the tongue easily at my house is "Oh, brother" (according to my daughter).

I'd gladly roll out the welcome mat for anybody who wants to visit. Come on over!

To round out my sewing basics of a ruler, mat, rotary cutter, and scissors, I'd add diagonal seam tape or Clearly Perfect Angles to avoid marking those pesky diagonal lines to make half-square triangles, flying geese, and Snowball block corners.

I'd roll out the red carpet for the person who invented coffee. That one cup in the morning is just lovely.

When I let the good times roll, I'm sure to have fun and laughter!

I just roll with it when things don't go according to plan. Maybe it will work out next time, and if not, the third time's a charm!

My no-longer-stray cats have me wrapped around their little paws. But don't tell any more of them!

When I'm making the rounds at local quilt shops, I make sure to chat with the shop owners and customers. Quilters are such a fun bunch.

In my home, we tend to gather 'round the living room for evening family time.

Ask around and my friends will tell you I'm trustworthy.

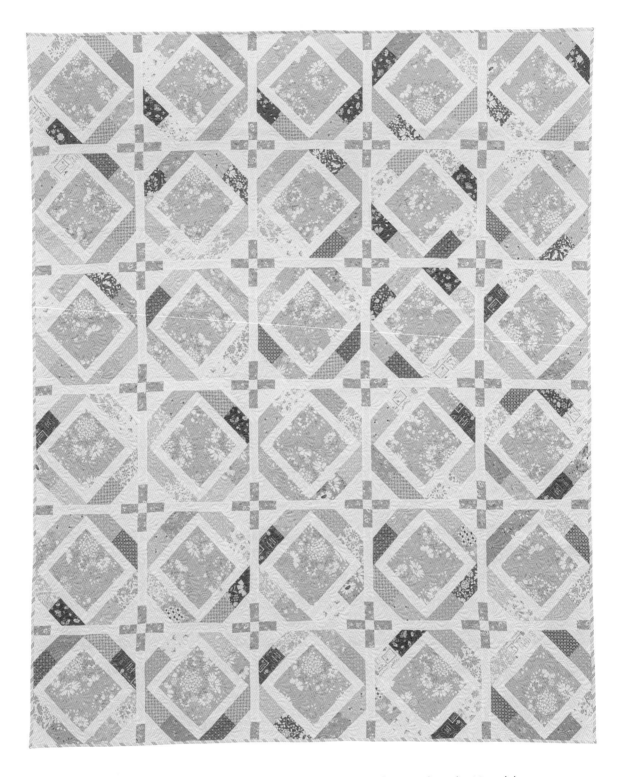

Designed by Corey Yoder; pieced by Corey Yoder and Jody Hershberger; quilted by David Hurd

2 Join five blocks and four sashing strips to make a block row. Make six rows measuring 12½" × 64½", including seam allowances.

3 Join five sashing strips and four white 1½" squares to make a sashing row. Make five rows measuring 1½" × 64½", including seam allowances.

4 Join the block rows alternately with the sashing rows. The quilt top should measure 64½" × 77½".

FINISHING THE QUILT

For more details on any finishing steps, visit ShopMartingale.com/HowtoQuilt for free downloadable information.

1 Layer the quilt top with batting and backing; baste the layers together.

2 Quilt by hand or machine. Corey's quilt is machine quilted with an allover design of plumes and swirls.

3 Use the striped 2½"-wide strips to make binding and then attach the binding to the quilt.

Quilt assembly

Jelly Cats

We've been keeping tabs on these tabby cats and can tell you they're practically purrrfect in every way. No two are exactly alike, and we wouldn't have it any other way. Just know, they've got their button eyes on you too!

FINISHED QUILT: 52½" × 52½" | FINISHED BLOCK: 10" × 10"

MATERIALS

Yardage is based on 42"-wide fabric; Jelly Rolls contain 40 strips, 2½" × width of fabric. Anne used Balboa by Sherri & Chelsi.

- 1 Jelly Roll of assorted prints for blocks, middle border, and outer border
- 1¾ yards of white solid for blocks, inner border, and outer border
- ½ yard of gray print for binding
- 3⅓ yards of fabric for backing
- 59" × 59" piece of batting
- 10 black buttons, ¼" diameter, for eyes
- Water-soluble marker or fabric pencil
- Freezer paper
- Light box (optional)

CUTTING

For the cat appliqués and the middle border, choose 15 Jelly Roll strips that blend together; set the strips aside for step 1 of "Making the Cat Blocks" on page 38. Choose 10 light or medium Jelly Roll strips for the sashing. Choose 2 coordinating strips for the outer-border corners. All measurements include ¼" seam allowances.

From the 10 light or medium print strips for sashing, cut a *total* of:
24 strips, 2½" × 10½"
16 squares, 2½" × 2½"

From *each* of the 2 strips for outer-border blocks, cut:
8 squares, 2½" × 2½" (16 total)

From the remaining assorted print strips, cut a *total* of:
4 rectangles, 2½" × 8½"
8 rectangles, 2½" × 6½"
4 rectangles, 2½" × 4½"
16 squares, 2½" × 2½"

From the *lengthwise* grain of the white solid, cut:
4 strips, 4½" × 44½"
2 strips, 2½" × 42½"
2 strips, 2½" × 38½"

From the remaining white solid, cut:
5 squares, 10½" × 10½"
8 strips, 1½" × 10½"
8 strips, 1½" × 8½"

From the gray print, cut:
6 strips, 2½" × 42"

MAKING THE CAT BLOCKS

Anne used machine appliqué and the instructions are written for that method, but use your favorite method if you prefer. The cat pattern is on page 43. Press seam allowances in the directions indicated by the arrows.

1 Using the Jelly Roll strips set aside for the cats, join five different 2½"-wide strips along their long edges to make a strip set. Make three strip sets measuring 10½" × 42", including seam allowances.

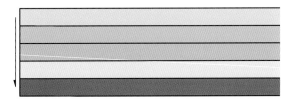

Make 3 strip sets,
10½" × 42".

2 Trace the cat pattern onto freezer paper and cut out the shape directly on the line. Cut out two facing right and three facing left. Use a hot, dry iron to press each freezer-paper template to the wrong side of the strip sets. Cut out each cat, adding a seam allowance of approximately ¼" all around. Set aside the remainders of the strip sets for the middle border.

3 Using the tip of your iron, press the seam allowance under along the edges of the freezer paper. Carefully remove the freezer paper and press edges again.

4 Center a cat on a white solid square, placing the bottom of the cat about 1" from the edge of the square. Pin or baste in place. Stitch by machine using a blind stitch or narrow zigzag stitch.

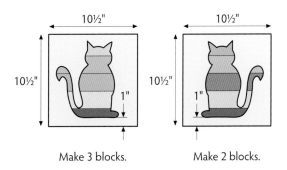

Make 3 blocks.   Make 2 blocks.

MAKING THE FRAMED FOUR PATCH BLOCKS

1 Lay out four print 2½" squares in two rows of two. Sew the squares into rows. Join the rows to make a four-patch unit. Make four units measuring 4½" square, including seam allowances.

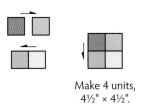

Make 4 units,
4½" × 4½".

2 Sew a print 2½" × 4½" rectangle to the right edge of a four-patch unit. Sew a print 2½" × 6½" rectangle to the top edge and another to the left edge of the unit. Sew a print 2½" × 8½" rectangle to the bottom of the unit. Make four units measuring 8½" square, including seam allowances.

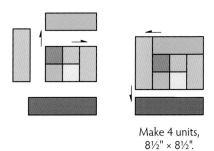

Make 4 units,
8½" × 8½".

3 Sew white solid 1½" × 8½" strips to opposite sides of a unit from step 2. Sew white solid 1½" × 10½" strips to the top and bottom edges to make a block. Make four blocks measuring 10½" square, including seam allowances.

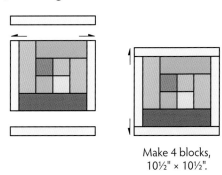

Make 4 blocks,
10½" × 10½".

ASSEMBLING THE QUILT TOP

Refer to the quilt assembly diagram below as needed throughout, noting the placement and orientation of the Cat and Framed Four Patch blocks.

1 Join four 2½" sashing squares and three 2½" × 10½" sashing strips to make a sashing row. Make four rows measuring 2½" × 38½", including seam allowances.

2 Join four 2½" × 10½" sashing strips and three blocks to make a block row. Make three rows measuring 10½" × 38½", including seam allowances. Notice that two of the rows have two Cats and one Framed Four Patch block and one row has one Cat and two Framed Four Patch blocks.

3 Join the sashing rows alternately with the block rows. The quilt-top center should measure 38½" square, including seam allowances.

ADDING THE BORDERS

1 Sew the white 2½" × 38½" strips to opposite sides of the quilt top. Sew the white 2½" × 42½" strips to the top and bottom edges. The quilt top should measure 42½" square, including seam allowances.

2 From the strip sets left over from step 1 of "Making the Cat Blocks," cut 20 segments, 1½" × 10½".

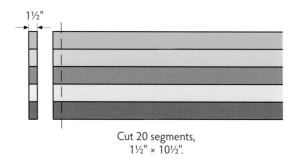

Cut 20 segments,
1½" × 10½".

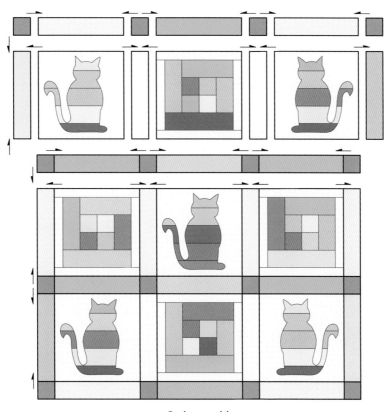

Quilt assembly

Designed and pieced by Anne Sutton; quilted by Rebecca Hubel

3 To make the middle border, join five segments end to end to make a border strip. Make four strips. For the side borders, remove four rectangles from one end to make a strip measuring 1½" × 42½", including seam allowances. Make two side borders. For the top border, remove three rectangles from one end to make a strip measuring 1½" × 44½", including seam allowances. Repeat to make the bottom border. Discard the extra rectangles or save them for use in another project.

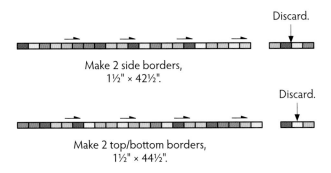

Discard.

Make 2 side borders,
1½" × 42½".

Discard.

Make 2 top/bottom borders,
1½" × 44½".

4 Sew the shorter middle borders to opposite sides of the quilt top. Sew the longer middle borders to the top and bottom edges. The quilt top should measure 44½" square, including seam allowances.

ROLLIN' WITH
Anne Sutton

BunnyHillDesigns.com

I'd like to give a round of applause to quilters who actually quilt my quilts! Without them, I'd have a whole bunch of flat-looking quilts.

To start the ball rolling on a new project, I clean my studio first, or it will drive me crazy.

One phrase that rolls off the tongue easily at my house is "What do you want for dinner?" My husband starts thinking about it in the morning. He does most of the microwaving (thought I'd say "cooking," didn't you?).

I'd gladly roll out the welcome mat for Covid-free friends to stitch with right now.

To round out my sewing basics of a ruler, mat, rotary cutter, and scissors, I'd add a wonderful wool pincushion.

I'd roll out the red carpet for the person who invented Ugg slippers.

I roll into my sewing room around 5 a.m., and you'll find me at my best. I'm such a morning person!

When I let the good times roll, I'm sure to have some stitching to do and a good show to watch.

I just roll with it whenever I can, though I have to remind myself sometimes.

My Chelsea dog has me wrapped around her little paw.

When I'm making the rounds at local quilt shops, I make sure to check out all the new fabrics. I can always make room for more.

Ask around and my friends will tell you I'm not as funny as I think I am.

41

⑤ For the outer-border corners, lay out four print 2½" squares in two rows of two. Sew the squares into rows. Join the rows to make a unit. Make four units measuring 4½" square, including seam allowances.

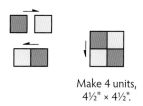

Make 4 units,
4½" × 4½".

⑥ Sew white solid 4½" × 44½" strips to opposite sides of the quilt top. Sew a corner unit from step 5 to each end of a white solid 4½" × 44½" strip. Make two and sew them to the top and bottom edges. The quilt top should measure 52½" square.

FINISHING THE QUILT

For more details on any finishing steps, visit ShopMartingale.com/HowtoQuilt for free downloadable information.

① Layer the quilt top with batting and backing; baste the layers together.

② Quilt by hand or machine. Anne's quilt is machine quilted with floral and leaf motifs in the blocks. Loops are stitched in the sashing and inner border. Ribbon candy and straight lines are stitched in the outer border.

③ Use the gray 2½"-wide strips to make binding and then attach the binding to the quilt. Referring to the pattern on page 43, attach buttons to each cat for eyes, or if the quilt is for a young child, embroider the eyes to avoid a chocking hazard.

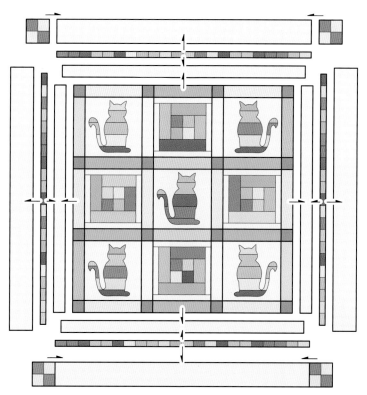

Adding the borders

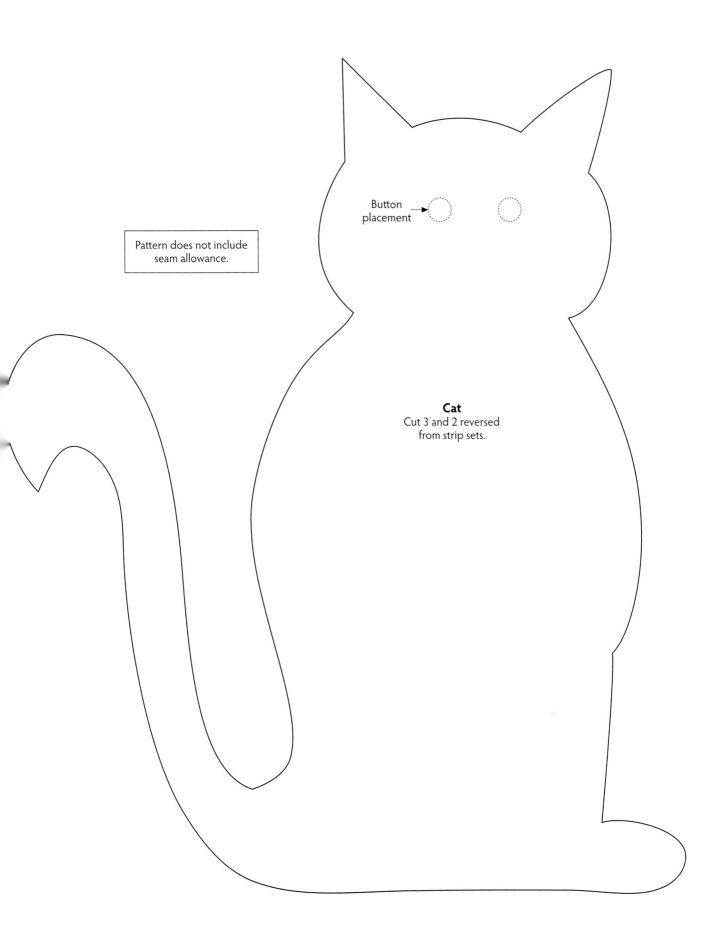

Button placement

Pattern does not include seam allowance.

Cat
Cut 3 and 2 reversed
from strip sets.

Out for a Spin

Scrappy stars catch most of the attention on a playful throw, but a closer look reveals that low-volume 16-Patch blocks have come along for the ride, adding their own subtle pizzazz.

FINISHED QUILT: 63½" × 71½" | FINISHED BLOCK: 8" × 8"

MATERIALS

Yardage is based on 42"-wide fabric; Jelly Rolls contain 40 strips, 2½" × width of fabric. Joanna used Figs & Shirtings by Fig Tree & Co.

- 1 Jelly Roll of assorted medium and dark prints (referred to collectively as "dark") for Star blocks*
- 1 Jelly Roll of assorted light prints for 16-Patch blocks*
- 2½ yards of ivory solid for blocks and setting squares
- ⅞ yard of blue print for border
- ⅝ yard of yellow floral for binding
- 4 yards of fabric for backing
- 70" × 78" piece of batting

*If the Jelly Roll contains 20 dark and 20 light strips, you'll only need 1 Jelly Roll.

CUTTING

As you cut the dark strips, keep like pieces together. All measurements include ¼" seam allowances.

From *each* of 19 assorted dark strips, cut:
2 rectangles, 2½" × 4½" (38 total)
12 squares, 2½" × 2½" (228 total)

From the ivory solid, cut:
15 strips, 2½" × 42"; crosscut into:
    76 rectangles, 2½" × 4½"
    76 squares, 2½" × 2½"
5 strips, 8½" × 42"; crosscut into 18 squares,
    8½" × 8½"

From the blue print, cut:
7 strips, 4" × 42"

From the yellow floral, cut:
7 strips, 2½" × 42"

MAKING THE STAR BLOCKS

For each block, select four squares and two rectangles from one dark print and label them A. Select eight squares from a different dark print and label them B. You'll also need four ivory rectangles and four ivory squares. Directions are for making one block. Repeat to make a total of 19 blocks. Press seam allowances in the directions indicated by the arrows.

1 Draw a diagonal line from corner to corner on the wrong side of the A and B squares. Place a marked A square on one end of an ivory rectangle, right sides together. Sew on the marked line. Trim the excess corner fabric ¼" from the stitched line. Place a marked A square on the opposite end of the ivory rectangle. Sew and trim as before to make a flying-geese unit measuring 2½" × 4½", including seam allowances. Make two A units. Repeat to make two B units using the marked B squares.

Make 2 A units, 2½" × 4½".   Make 2 B units, 2½" × 4½".

2 Repeat step 1 using the remaining marked B squares and the A rectangles to make two A/B flying-geese units.

Make 2 A/B units, 2½" × 4½".

3 Join two A/B flying-geese units to make a center unit measuring 4½" square, including seam allowances.

Make 1 unit, 4½" × 4½".

4 Lay out the A and B flying-geese units from step 1, four ivory squares, and the center unit in three rows of three, making sure to place like fabrics together. Sew the pieces into rows. Join the rows to make a block measuring 8½" square, including seam allowances. Repeat the steps to make a total of 19 blocks.

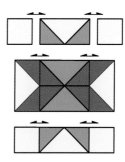 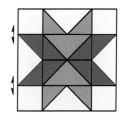

Make 19 blocks, 8½" × 8½".

MAKING THE 16-PATCH BLOCKS

1 Join four assorted light strips to make a strip set measuring 8½" × 42", including seam allowances. Make five strip sets. Cut the strip sets into 76 segments, 2½" × 8½".

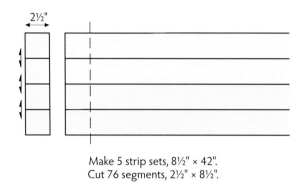

Make 5 strip sets, 8½" × 42".
Cut 76 segments, 2½" × 8½".

2 Join four assorted segments to make a block measuring 8½" square, including seam allowances. Make 19 blocks.

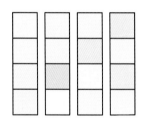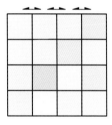

Make 19 blocks,
8½" × 8½".

Pressing Matters

When making the 16-Patch blocks, sew the light patchwork strips in alternating directions to avoid distortion. Press them in pairs as you go (rather than waiting until all four strips are sewn together) in order to get a good press.

ROLLIN' WITH
Joanna Figueroa

FigTreeandCompany.com

I'd like to give a round of applause to quilters who do all of their own quilting. It's a skill I admire. Each time I try it, I admire those who quilt so much more!

To start the ball rolling on a new project, I organize my entire study, often even the parts completely unrelated to the new project. It helps clear my mind while I ponder the new design.

One phrase that rolls off the tongue easily at my house is "Let's figure it out." We're big proponents of figuring things out together. I wonder if that's why I enjoy designing—plenty to figure out there!

To round out my sewing basics of a ruler, mat, rotary cutter, and scissors, I'd add my favorite pins and pincushion. Don't leave home without them.

I'd roll out the red carpet for the person who invented pumpkin-spice anything. It's the perfect blend of fall goodness!

When I let the good times roll, I'm sure to have '80s music playing and a good movie marathon on in the background. OK, and maybe some dark chocolate and a good cup of tea by my side too.

I just roll with it when pieces don't quite match. I'm not much of a seam ripper unless it's really necessary! Quilting is supposed to be a fun craft, not a precision work of art in my humble opinion.

My chickens **have me wrapped around their little feet (?).** I feel like I work harder to make sure they get their treats than I do for the dog or cat.

Ask around and my friends will tell you I'm always dreaming up a new project. I'm trying to learn how to slow down more and enjoy what's in front of me.

Designed by Joanna Figueroa; pieced by Cheryl Hadley and Joanna Figueroa;
quilted by Marion Bott

ASSEMBLING THE QUILT TOP

1 Lay out the Star blocks, 16-Patch blocks, and ivory squares in eight rows of seven as shown in the quilt assembly diagram below. Sew the pieces into rows. Join the rows to make the quilt-top center, which should measure 56½" × 64½", including seam allowances.

2 Join the blue 4"-wide strips end to end. From the pieced strip, cut two 64½"-long strips and two 63½"-long strips. Sew the longer strips to opposite sides of the quilt center. Sew the shorter strips to the top and bottom edges to complete the quilt top. The quilt top should measure 63½" × 71½".

FINISHING THE QUILT

For more details on any finishing steps, visit ShopMartingale.com/HowtoQuilt for free downloadable information.

1 Layer the quilt top with batting and backing; baste the layers together.

2 Quilt by hand or machine. Joanna's quilt is machine quilted with an allover sand-dollar design.

3 Use the yellow 2½"-wide strips to make binding and then attach the binding to the quilt.

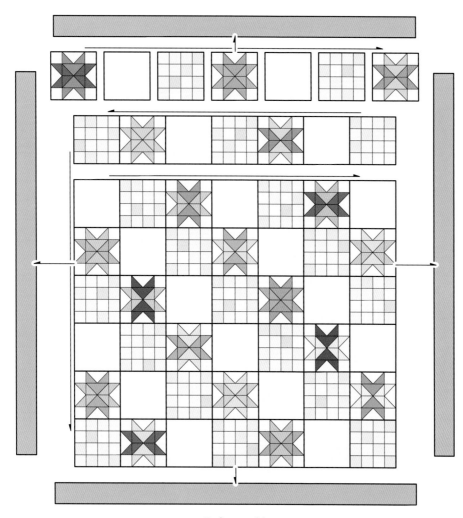

Quilt assembly

Plus Side

What's better than one Jelly Roll? How about two Jelly Rolls!
They're the winning combination when it comes to creating a positively
gorgeous quilt that blends plus signs in a roundabout way!

FINISHED QUILT: 67½" × 67½" | **FINISHED BLOCK: 9" × 9"**

MATERIALS

Yardage is based on 42"-wide fabric; Jelly Rolls contain
40 strips, 2½" × width of fabric. Sherri used Happy Days
by Sherri & Chelsi.

- 2 matching Jelly Rolls of assorted dark
  and light prints for blocks
- 2⅜ yards of white solid for blocks and
  setting triangles
- 1⅛ yards of white print for sashing and
  inner border
- ⅛ yard of gray print for sashing squares
- ⅞ yard of aqua floral for outer border
- ⅝ yard of pink stripe for binding
- 4⅛ yards of fabric for backing
- 74" × 74" piece of batting

CUTTING

All measurements include ¼" seam allowances.

From *each of 25* assorted dark strips, cut:
1 square, 2½" × 2½" (25 total)
2 rectangles, 2" × 9½" (50 total)
2 rectangles, 2" × 6½" (50 total)

From *each of 25* assorted dark strips, cut:
4 squares, 2½" × 2½" (100 total)

From *each of 4* assorted light strips, cut:
12 squares, 2½" × 2½" (48 total)

From the white solid, cut:
10 strips, 3½" × 42"; crosscut into 100 squares,
  3½" × 3½"
4 strips, 2½" × 42"; crosscut into 52 squares,
  2½" × 2½"
2 strips, 15½" × 42"; crosscut into:
  3 squares, 15½" × 15½"; cut the squares into
    quarters diagonally to yield 12 side triangles
  2 squares, 8⅞" × 8⅞"; cut the squares in half
    diagonally to yield 4 corner triangles

From the white print, cut:
23 strips, 1½" × 42"; crosscut *16 of the strips* into
  64 strips, 1½" × 9½"

From the gray print, cut:
2 strips, 1½" × 42"; crosscut into 40 squares,
  1½" × 1½"

From the aqua floral, cut:
7 strips, 4" × 42"

From the pink stripe, cut:
7 strips, 2½" × 42"

MAKING THE BLOCKS

Press seam allowances in the directions indicated by the arrows.

1 Lay out four matching dark squares, four matching light (or white solid) squares, and one contrasting dark square in three rows of three. Sew the squares into rows. Join the rows to make a nine-patch unit. Make 25 units measuring 6½" square, including seam allowances.

Make 25 units,
6½" × 6½".

2 Using dark rectangles that match the center square, sew dark 2" × 6½" rectangles to opposite sides of a nine-patch unit. Sew dark 2" × 9½" rectangles to the top and bottom edges. Make 25 units measuring 9½" square, including seam allowances.

Make 25 units,
9½" × 9½".

3 Draw a diagonal line from corner to corner on the wrong side of each white solid 3½" square. Place marked squares on the corners of a unit from step 2. Sew on the marked lines. Trim the excess corner fabric ¼" from the stitched lines. Make 25 blocks measuring 9½" square, including seam allowances.

ASSEMBLING THE QUILT TOP

1 Lay out the blocks, white print 1½" × 9½" strips, gray squares, and white solid side and corner triangles in diagonal rows as shown in the quilt assembly diagram below. Join the white strips and gray squares to make sashing rows. Sew the blocks and white strips into rows to make block rows. Sew a sashing row to the top of each appropriate block row, and then add the side triangles. Join the rows, adding the corner triangles last.

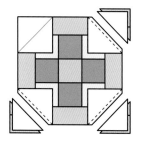 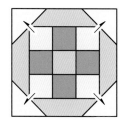

Make 25 blocks,
9½" × 9½".

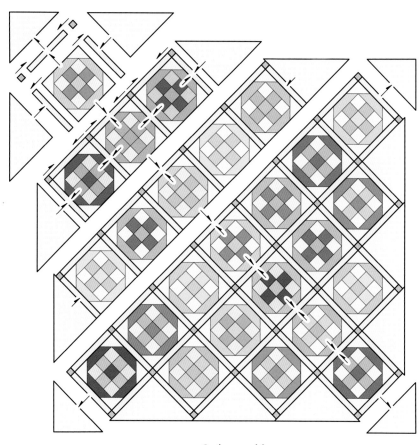

Quilt assembly

Designed and pieced by Sherri L. McConnell; quilted by Marion Bott

2 Trim and square up the quilt top, making sure to leave ¼" beyond the points of all gray squares for seam allowances. The quilt-top center should measure 58½" square, including seam allowances.

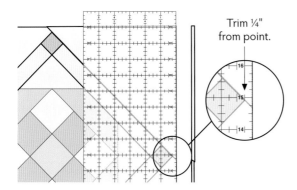

Trim ¼" from point.

3 Join the remaining white print strips end to end. From the pieced strip, cut two 60½"-long strips and two 58½"-long strips. Sew the shorter strips to opposite sides of the quilt center. Sew the longer strips to the top and bottom edges to complete the inner border. Press all seam allowances toward the border. The quilt top should measure 60½" square, including seam allowances.

4 Join the aqua strips end to end. From the pieced strip, cut two 67½"-long strips and two 60½"-long strips. Sew the shorter strips to opposite sides of the quilt top. Sew the longer strips to the top and bottom edges to complete the quilt top. Press all seam allowances toward the outer border. The quilt top should measure 67½" square.

FINISHING THE QUILT

For more details on any finishing steps, visit ShopMartingale.com/HowtoQuilt for free downloadable information.

1 Layer the quilt top with batting and backing; baste the layers together.

2 Quilt by hand or machine. Sherri's quilt is machine quilted with an allover design of curved lines.

3 Use the pink 2½"-wide strips to make binding and then attach the binding to the quilt.

ROLLIN' WITH
Sherri L. McConnell

AQuiltingLife.com

I'd like to give a round of applause to quilters who clean up their work space after every project. ☺

To start the ball rolling on a new project, I clean up my work space!

One phrase that rolls off the tongue easily at my house is "It'll be alright."

I'd gladly roll out the welcome mat for a personal chef and housekeeper.

To round out my sewing basics of a ruler, mat, rotary cutter, and scissors, I'd add a seam ripper!

I'd roll out the red carpet for the person who invented lobster bisque.

I roll into my sewing room around 8 p.m. and I'm closing up for the night.

When I let the good times roll, I'm sure to have lots of laughs!

I just roll with it when I make a mistake.

My cute grandkids have me wrapped around their little fingers.

When I'm making the rounds at local quilt shops, I make sure to enjoy the displays and fabrics and look for new notions.

In my home, we tend to gather 'round the fire. We just added a fun fire pit to our backyard for visiting—and of course making s'mores!

Ask around and my friends will tell you I'm always saying, "I'll be caught up after I finish this quilt."

Sit a Spell

The comfort of sitting down with a quilt and cup of tea can equal the comfort found in time spent sewing. As your quilt comes together, linger over your favorite fabrics and imagine where you'll enjoy your latest creation.

FINISHED QUILT: 60½" × 73⅛" | **FINISHED BLOCK: 9" × 9"**

MATERIALS

Yardage is based on 42"-wide fabric; Jelly Rolls contain 40 strips, 2½" × width of fabric. Vanessa used Folktale by Lella Boutique.

- 1 Jelly Roll of assorted prints for blocks
- 2⅝ yards of gold stripe for blocks
- 2 yards of rose print for setting triangles and border
- ⅝ yard of gold print for binding
- 4½ yards of fabric for backing
- 67" × 80" piece of batting

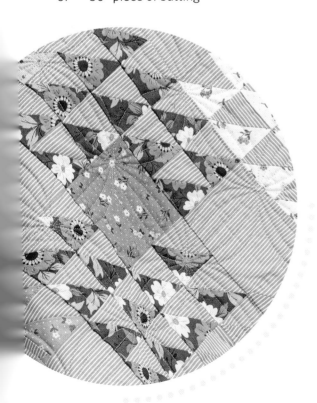

CUTTING

All measurements include ¼" seam allowances.

From *each* of 32 assorted print strips, cut:
12 squares, 2½" × 2½" (384 total)
2 rectangles, 2" × 3½" (64 total; see "Extra Strips" on page 58)

From the gold stripe, cut:
26 strips, 2½" × 42"; crosscut into 384 squares, 2½" × 2½"
6 strips, 3½" × 42"; crosscut into 64 squares, 3½" × 3½"

From the rose print, cut:
2 strips, 14" × 42"; crosscut into:
    4 squares, 14" × 14"; cut the squares into quarters diagonally to yield 16 side triangles (2 are extra)
    2 squares, 7⅜" × 7⅜"; cut the squares in half diagonally to yield 4 corner triangles
7 strips, 5" × 42"

From the gold print, cut:
7 strips, 2½" × 42"

Extra Strips

You can cut additional pairs of 2" × 3½" rectangles from the eight leftover Jelly Roll strips. Substitute these rectangles for any of the print rectangles listed in "Cutting" on page 57 that you don't want to use in the center of your blocks.

MAKING THE BLOCKS

Press seam allowances in the directions indicated by the arrows.

1 Draw a diagonal line from corner to corner on the wrong side of the gold stripe 2½" squares. Layer a marked square on a print square, right sides together. Sew ¼" from both sides of the line. Cut the unit apart on the line to make two half-square-triangle units. Trim to 2" square, including seam allowances. Make 32 sets of 24 matching units.

Make 32 sets of
24 matching units.

2 Lay out eight matching half-square-triangle units in two rows of four, orienting the units as shown. Sew the units into rows, and then join the rows. Make 32 sets of two matching units measuring 3½" × 6½", including seam allowances.

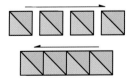 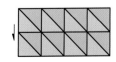

Make 32 sets of 2 matching units,
3½" × 6½".

3 Lay out four matching half-square-triangle units in two rows of two, orienting the units as shown. Sew the units into rows, and then join the rows. Make 32 sets of two matching units measuring 3½" square, including seam allowances.

Make 32 sets of 2 matching units,
3½" × 3½".

4 Join two matching print rectangles to make a center unit. Make 32 units measuring 3½" square, including seam allowances.

Make 32 units,
3½" × 3½".

5 Lay out two units each from steps 2 and 3, all matching; two gold stripe 3½" squares; and one center unit from step 4, noting the orientation of the units. Sew the pieces into rows. Join the rows to make a block. Make 32 blocks measuring 9½" square, including seam allowances.

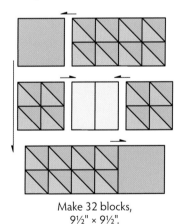

Make 32 blocks,
9½" × 9½".

Designed and pieced by Vanessa Goertzen; quilted by Kaitlyn Howell

ASSEMBLING THE QUILT TOP

1 Lay out the blocks and rose side triangles in eight diagonal rows as shown in the quilt assembly diagram. Sew the pieces into rows. Join the rows, and then add the rose corner triangles.

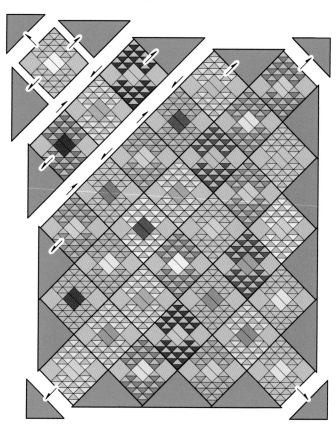

2 Trim and square up the quilt top, making sure to leave ¼" beyond the points of all blocks for seam allowances. The quilt-top center should measure 51½" × 64⅛", including seam allowances.

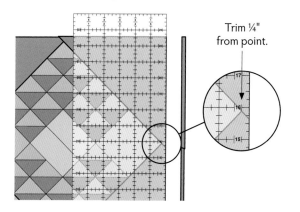

Trim ¼" from point.

3 Join the rose 5"-wide strips end to end. From the pieced strip, cut two 64⅛"-long strips and two 60½"-long strips. Sew the longer strips to opposite sides of the quilt center. Sew the shorter strips to the top and bottom edges. Press all seam allowances toward the border strips. The quilt top should measure 60½" × 73⅛".

FINISHING THE QUILT

For more details on any finishing steps, visit ShopMartingale.com/HowtoQuilt for free downloadable information.

1 Layer the quilt top with batting and backing; baste the layers together.

2 Quilt by hand or machine. Vanessa's quilt is machine quilted with an allover double pumpkin seed motif.

3 Use the gold print 2½"-wide strips to make binding and then attach the binding to the quilt.

ROLLIN' WITH
Vanessa Goertzen

LellaBoutique.com

I'd like to give a round of applause to quilters who save scraps. I'm a minimalist, and I don't like storing them.

To start the ball rolling on a new project, I like to look at the fabric and contemplate its personality. I wonder what kind of shapes it would want to be made into.

I'd gladly roll out the welcome mat for anyone bringing treats.

To round out my sewing basics of a ruler, mat, rotary cutter, and scissors, I'd add my Bernina 550 QE.

I'd roll out the red carpet for the person who invented long-arm quilting.

When I let the good times roll, I'm sure to have a dangly pair of earrings on. The bigger the better!

In my home, we tend to gather 'round board games and snacks.

True North

If you love rainbows and ombré, you're definitely headed in the right direction with this spectacular array of Flying Geese. Whether its final destination is as a baby quilt, wall hanging, or small lap quilt, all signs point to a happy day.

FINISHED QUILT: 48½" × 54½"

MATERIALS

Yardage is based on 42"-wide fabric; Jelly Rolls contain 40 strips, 2½" × width of fabric. Vanessa used Ombre Fairy Dust by V & Co.

- 1 Jelly Roll of assorted prints for flying-geese units*
- 3⅜ yards of white print for flying-geese units
- ½ yard of black print for binding
- 3⅛ yards of fabric for backing
- 55" × 61" piece of batting

*Vanessa used an Ombre Fairy Dust Jelly Roll with 1 strip each of 28 colors in yellow, orange, red, magenta, and purple and 2 strips each of pink, teal, green, and gray. She did not use the 2 white and 2 black strips from the Jelly Roll.

CUTTING

All measurements include ¼" seam allowances.

From *each of 36* assorted print strips, cut:
9 rectangles, 2½" × 4½" (324 total)

From the white print, cut:
44 strips, 2½" × 42"; crosscut into 648 squares, 2½" × 2½"

From the black print, cut:
6 strips, 2½" × 42"

ASSEMBLING THE QUILT TOP

Press seam allowances in the directions indicated by the arrows.

1 Draw a diagonal line from corner to corner on the wrong side of the white squares. Place a marked square on one end of a print rectangle, right sides together. Sew on the line. Trim the excess corner fabric ¼" from the stitched line. Place a marked square on the opposite end of the rectangle. Sew and trim as before to make a flying-geese unit measuring 2½" × 4½", including seam allowances. Make 324 units, keeping like colors together.

Make 324 units, 2½" × 4½".

2 Starting in the upper-left corner with the yellow units, lay out the units in 27 rows of 12 units each as shown in the quilt assembly diagram on page 65 and the quilt photo on page 64. Working diagonally to the lower-right corner, add the orange, red, and pink units. Continue with the magenta, purple, teal, green, and gray units.

Designed and pieced by Vanessa Christenson; quilted by Megan Pitz

3 Sew the units into rows. Join the rows to complete the quilt top. The quilt top should measure 48½" × 54½".

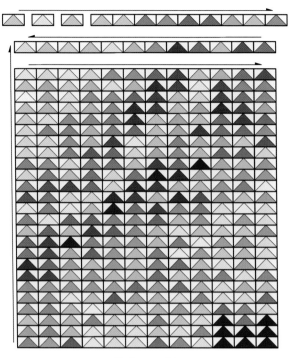

Quilt assembly

FINISHING THE QUILT

For more details on any finishing steps, visit ShopMartingale.com/HowtoQuilt for free downloadable information.

1 Layer the quilt top with batting and backing; baste the layers together.

2 Quilt by hand or machine. Vanessa's quilt is machine quilted with parallel horizontal wavy lines.

3 Use the black 2½"-wide strips to make binding and then attach the binding to the quilt.

ROLLIN' WITH
Vanessa Christenson

VanessaChristenson.com

I'd like to give a round of applause to quilters who roll with the punches!

To start the ball rolling on a new project, I get a great television series on queue!

One phrase that rolls off the tongue easily at my house is "Where's the dark chocolate?"

I'd gladly roll out the welcome mat for anyone bringing dark chocolate and laughter!

To round out my sewing basics of a ruler, mat, rotary cutter, and scissors, I'd add starch!

I'd roll out the red carpet for the person who invented quilting bees.

I roll into my sewing room around mid-afternoon after an outdoor workout.

When I let the good times roll, I'm sure to have friends around.

I just roll with it when plans don't go as planned.

My family has me wrapped around their little fingers.

When I'm making the rounds at local quilt shops, I make sure to look at all the cute embroidery scissors.

In my home, we tend to gather 'round the kitchen.

Ask around and my friends will tell you I'm a lot of punch in a small package.

Bear Necessities

Is it necessary to hum "the simple, bare necessities" as you piece the scrappy Bear Paw blocks? We can't be sure. But we are certain that you'll rest at ease under a comforting quilt when you're finished!

FINISHED QUILT: 52½" × 66" | FINISHED BLOCKS: 10½" × 10½" and 3" × 3"

MATERIALS

Yardage is based on 42"-wide fabric; Jelly Rolls contain 40 strips, 2½" × width of fabric. Sandy used Sweet Harmony by American Jane.

- 1 Jelly Roll of assorted prints for blocks and border
- 3½ yards of cream print for blocks and borders
- ⅝ yard of navy print for binding
- 3⅓ yards of fabric for backing
- 59" × 72" piece of batting

CUTTING

All measurements include ¼" seam allowances.

From the assorted print strips, cut a *total* of:
234 squares, 2½" × 2½"
204 squares, 2" × 2"

From the cream print, cut:
22 strips, 2½" × 42"; crosscut *16 of the strips* into 234
    squares, 2½" × 2½"
9 strips, 2" × 42"; crosscut into:
    48 rectangles, 2" × 5"
    48 squares, 2" × 2"
6 strips, 3" × 42"; crosscut into:
    3 strips, 3" × 37"
    8 strips, 3" × 11"
3 strips, 3½" × 42"
3 strips, 3¼" × 42"

From the navy print, cut:
7 strips, 2½" × 42"

MAKING THE BLOCKS

Press seam allowances in the directions indicated by the arrows.

1. Draw a diagonal line from corner to corner on the wrong side of the cream 2½" squares. Layer a marked square on a print 2½" square, right sides together. Sew ¼" from both sides of the drawn line. Cut the unit apart on the marked line to make two half-square-triangle units. Trim the units to measure 2" square, including seam allowances. Make 468 units.

Make 468 units.

the pieces into rows. Join the rows to make a block. Make 12 blocks measuring 11" square, including seam allowances.

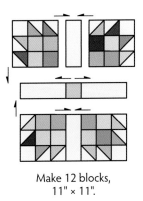

Make 12 blocks,
11" × 11".

② Lay out four different print 2" squares in two rows of two squares each. Sew the squares into rows and then join the rows to make a four-patch unit. Make 48 units measuring 3½" square, including seam allowances.

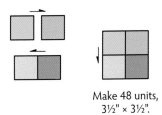

Make 48 units,
3½" × 3½".

③ Lay out four half-square-triangle units, one cream 2" square, and one four-patch unit as shown. Join two triangle units and then sew them to the left edge of the four-patch unit. Join two triangle units and the cream square to make a row. Sew the row to the top edge to make a corner unit. Make 48 units measuring 5" square, including seam allowances. Set aside the remaining triangle units to make the pieced border.

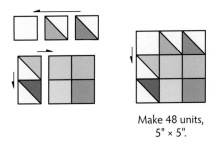

Make 48 units,
5" × 5".

④ Lay out four corner units, four cream rectangles, and one print 2" square in three rows, noting the orientation of the corner units. Sew

ASSEMBLING THE QUILT TOP

Refer to the quilt assembly diagram below as needed throughout.

① Join three blocks and two cream 3" × 11" strips to make a block row. Make four rows measuring 11" × 37", including seam allowances.

② Join the block rows alternately with the cream 3" × 37" strips. The quilt-top center should measure 37" × 50", including seam allowances.

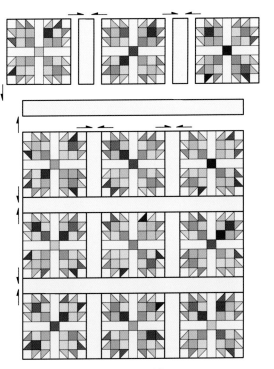

Quilt assembly

ADDING THE BORDERS

1 Join the cream 3¼"-wide strips end to end. From the pieced strip, cut two 50"-long strips. Sew the strips to opposite sides of the quilt center. Join the cream 3½"-wide strips end to end. From the pieced strip, cut two 42½"-long strips and sew them to the top and bottom edges. The quilt top should measure 42½" × 56", including seam allowances.

2 Lay out 37 half-square-triangle units with 19 units pointing to the right and 18 units pointing to the left. Join the units to make a border strip. Make two strips measuring 2" × 56", including seam allowances. Make two reversed strips with 19 units pointing to the left and 18 units pointing to the right. Join one strip and one reversed strip, rotating one strip as shown to form a diamond shape in the center. Make two side borders measuring 3½" × 56", including seam allowances.

Make 2 side borders,
3½" × 56".

3 Lay out 28 half-square-triangle units with 14 units pointing in one direction and 14 units pointing in the opposite direction. Join the units to make a border strip. Make four strips measuring 2" × 42½", including seam allowances. Join two

strips, rotating one strip to form a diamond shape in the center, to make the top border. The border should measure 3½" × 42½", including seam allowances. Repeat to make the bottom border.

Make 2 top/bottom units,
3½" × 42½".

4 Lay out four half-square-triangle units in two rows of two units each to form a pinwheel. Sew the units into rows and then join the rows to make a Pinwheel block. Make four blocks measuring 3½" square, including seam allowances.

Make 4 blocks,
3½" × 3½".

5 Sew the pieced side borders to opposite sides of the quilt top. Sew Pinwheel blocks to both ends of the top and bottom triangle borders. Sew these borders to the top and bottom edges. The quilt top should measure 48½" × 62", including seam allowances.

Designed, pieced, and quilted by Sandy Klop

6 Join the cream 2½"-wide strips end to end. From the pieced strip, cut two 62"-long strips and two 52½"-long strips. Sew the longer strips to opposite sides of the quilt top. Sew the shorter strips to the top and bottom edges to complete the quilt top. The quilt top should measure 52½" × 66".

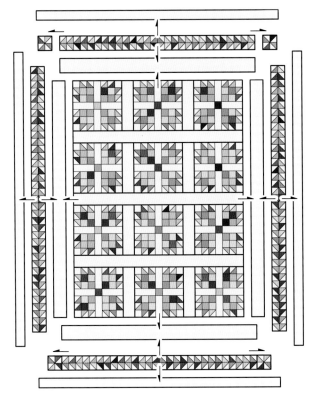

Adding the borders

FINISHING THE QUILT

For more details on any finishing steps, visit ShopMartingale.com/HowtoQuilt for free downloadable information.

1 Layer the quilt top with batting and backing; baste the layers together.

2 Quilt by hand or machine. Sandy's quilt is machine quilted with overall meandering.

3 Use the navy 2½"-wide strips to make binding and then attach the binding to the quilt.

ROLLIN' WITH
Sandy Klop
AmericanJane.com

I'd like to give a round of applause to quilters who use my patterns but then do a little something to make it their own.

To start the ball rolling on a new project, I gather my fabric to see who works and plays well with others.

One phrase that rolls off the tongue easily at my house is "We all get the same amount of time, it just depends what you do with it."

I'd gladly roll out the welcome mat for a Pembroke Welsh corgi puppy.

To round out my sewing basics of a ruler, mat, rotary cutter, and scissors, I'd add a clear surface!

I'd roll out the red carpet for the person who invented the rotary cutter.

I just roll with it when I'm doing a puzzle.

My grandchildren have me wrapped around their little fingers.

When I'm making the rounds at a local quilt shop, I...don't shop anymore since I have a house full of fabric!

In my home, we tend to gather 'round the kitchen table.

Ask around, my friends will tell you I'm happy!

Come Together

The success of a quilt can often been seen in the culmination of its diverse elements. What catches your eye—the vintage game-board style, the dark and light backgrounds, or the center stars? Together, they're magic!

FINISHED QUILT: 72½" × 72½" | **FINISHED BLOCK: 16" × 16"**

MATERIALS

Yardage is based on 42"-wide fabric; Jelly Rolls contain 40 strips, 2½" × width of fabric. April used Homestead by April Rosenthal.

- 1 Jelly Roll of assorted prints for blocks
- 3⅛ yards of white print for blocks and border
- 3¾ yards of gray print for blocks, border, and binding
- 4½ yards of fabric for backing
- 79" × 79" piece of batting
- 6½" square ruler with a 45° line

CUTTING

All measurements include ¼" seam allowances.

From *each* of 32 assorted print strips, cut:
2 strips, 1¼" × 42" (64 total)

From 7 assorted print strips, cut a *total* of:
32 rectangles, 2" × 8"

From the white print, cut:
9 strips, 2½" × 42"; crosscut into 128 squares,
     2½" × 2½"
4 strips, 7½" × 42"; crosscut into 16 squares,
     7½" × 7½"
2 strips, 4½" × 42"; crosscut into 10 squares,
     4½" × 4½"
12 strips, 2" × 42"; crosscut into:
     32 strips, 2" × 10"
     32 rectangles, 2" × 4"
1 strip, 16½" × 42"; crosscut into 8 strips, 4½" × 16½"

From the gray print, cut:
9 strips, 2½" × 42"; crosscut into 128 squares,
     2½" × 2½"
7 strips, 7½" × 42"; crosscut into 32 squares,
     7½" × 7½". Cut *16 of the squares* in half diagonally
     to yield 32 triangles.
2 strips, 4½" × 42"; crosscut into 10 squares,
     4½" × 4½"
1 strip, 16½" × 42"; crosscut into 8 strips, 4½" × 16½"
8 strips, 2½" × 42"

MAKING THE BLOCKS

Press seam allowances in the directions indicated by the arrows.

1 Sew eight assorted print 1¼"-wide strips together to make a strip set measuring 6½" × 42", including seam allowances. Make a total of eight strip sets. Cut the strip sets into 64 segments, 4½" × 6½".

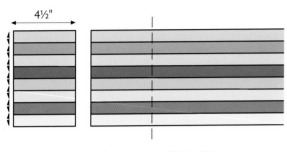

Make 8 strip sets, 6½" × 42".
Cut 64 segments, 4½" × 6½".

2 Draw a diagonal line from corner to corner on the wrong side of the white and gray 2½" squares. Place a white square on the bottom-left corner of a segment from step 1. Sew on the marked line. Trim the excess corner fabric ¼" from the stitched line. Place a white square on the bottom-right corner. Sew and trim as before. Repeat to sew gray squares to the two remaining corners to make a side unit. Make 64 units measuring 4½" × 6½", including seam allowances.

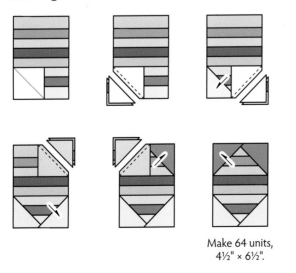

Make 64 units,
4½" × 6½".

3 Draw a diagonal line from corner to corner on the wrong side of the white 7½" squares. Layer a marked square on a gray 7½" square, right sides together. Sew ¼" from both sides of the drawn line. Cut the unit apart on the marked line to make two half-square-triangle units. Trim the units to measure 6½" square, including seam allowances. Make 32 units.

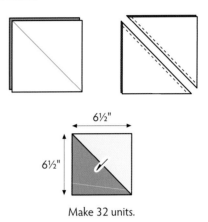

Make 32 units.

4 Fold a gray triangle in half and lightly crease to mark the center of the long side. Fold a white 2" × 10" strip, a print 2" × 8" strip, and a white 2" × 4" rectangle in half and lightly crease to mark the centers of their long sides. Center and sew the white strip to the long side of the triangle. Center and sew the print strip and then the white rectangle to the unit. Using a 6½" square ruler and placing the 45° line on the ruler on the center seamline, trim the unit to measure 6½" square, including seam allowances. Make 32 corner units.

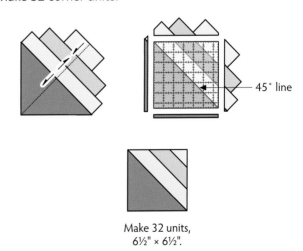

45° line

Make 32 units,
6½" × 6½".

5 Lay out four corner units, four side units, and one white 4½" square in three rows of three, rotating the side units to form a white star in the center. Sew the pieces into rows. Join the rows to make a block measuring 16½" square, including seam allowances. Make eight blocks with a white center star.

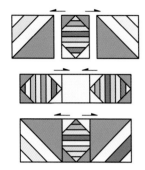
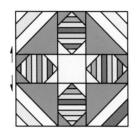

Make 8 white Star blocks,
16½" × 16½".

6 Lay out four half-square-triangle units, four side units, and one gray 4½" square in three rows of three, rotating the side units to form a gray star in the center. Sew the pieces into rows. Join the rows to make a block measuring 16½" square, including seam allowances. Make eight blocks with a gray center star.

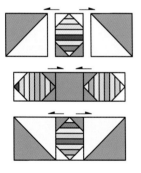
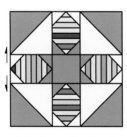

Make 8 gray Star blocks,
16½" × 16½".

ROLLIN' WITH
April Rosenthal

AprilRosenthal.com

I'd like to give a round of applause to quilters who try new things! I think it's awesome when people are constantly learning.

To start the ball rolling on a new project, I try to cut all the pieces out at the beginning and get super organized. This helps me stay motivated.

One phrase that rolls off the tongue easily at my house is "GOALLLLL!" We love soccer around here, and my older kids are both goal-scoring forwards.

I'd gladly roll out the welcome mat for the pizza delivery guy. Sometimes Mama needs to skip the cooking and keep sewing.

To round out my sewing basics of a ruler, mat, rotary cutter, and scissors, I'd add my old metal sewing machine. They don't make 'em like they used to!

I'd roll out the red carpet for the person who invented prefilled bobbins—they're the best ever.

When I let the good times roll, I'm sure to have music going in the background. There are always good tunes playing at my house.

My kids, for sure, **have me wrapped around their little fingers.** They know I'm the pushover parent when it comes to bedtimes.

When I'm making the rounds at local quilt shops, I make sure to buy something. I love supporting local quilt shops.

In my home, we tend to gather 'round the fireplace and play card games.

Ask around, my friends will tell you I'm snarky, independent, and well-researched.

Designed and pieced by April Rosenthal; quilted by Melissa Kelley

ASSEMBLING THE QUILT TOP

Refer to the quilt assembly diagram below as needed throughout.

1 Lay out the blocks in four rows of four blocks each, alternating them in each row and from row to row. Sew the blocks into rows and then join the rows to make the quilt-top center. The quilt center should measure 64½" square, including seam allowances.

2 Join two white and two gray 4½" × 16½" strips to make a side border measuring 4½" × 64½", including seam allowances. Make two. Make two more borders in the same way, but then add a white 4½" square to one end and a gray 4½" square to the other end. The top and bottom borders should measure 4½" × 72½", including seam allowances.

3 Sew the borders to opposite sides of the quilt top and then to the top and bottom edges. The quilt top should measure 72½" square.

FINISHING THE QUILT

For more details on any finishing steps, visit ShopMartingale.com/HowtoQuilt for free downloadable information.

1 Layer the quilt top with batting and backing; baste the layers together.

2 Quilt by hand or machine. April's quilt is machine quilted with an allover double clamshell design.

3 Use the gray 2½"-wide strips to make binding and then attach the binding to the quilt.

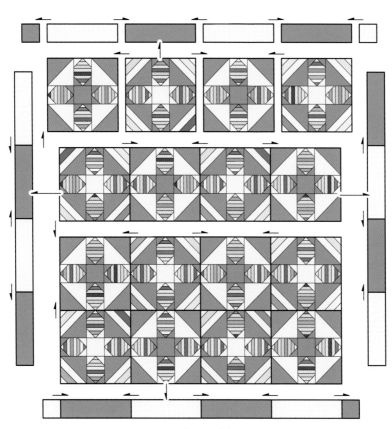

Quilt assembly

Family Gathering

Now more than ever, there's something special about gathering with family and friends. And for many, the heart of home is centered around watching our circle of family and friends grow, like adding pieces to a patchwork quilt.

FINISHED QUILT: 68½" × 68½"

MATERIALS

Yardage is based on 42"-wide fabric; Jelly Rolls contain 40 strips, 2½" × width of fabric. Lissa used Cider by Basic Grey.

- 2 Jelly Rolls of assorted prints in gold, navy, cream, blue, slate, orange, tan, and peach for quilt center and outer border
- ⅓ yard of coral print for inner border
- ⅜ yard of navy print for middle border
- ⅝ yard of navy dot for binding
- 4¼ yards of fabric for backing
- 75" × 75" piece of batting

CUTTING

All measurements include ¼" seam allowances.

From the gold strips, cut a *total* of:
72 rectangles, 2½" × 4½"
8 squares, 2½" × 2½"

From the navy strips, cut a *total* of:
52 rectangles, 2½" × 4½"
8 squares, 2½" × 2½"

From the cream strips, cut a *total* of:
52 rectangles, 2½" × 4½"
12 squares, 2½" × 2½"

From the blue strips, cut a *total* of:
60 rectangles, 2½" × 4½"
8 squares, 2½" × 2½"

From the slate strips, cut a *total* of:
60 rectangles, 2½" × 4½"
8 squares, 2½" × 2½"

From the orange strips, cut a *total* of:
36 rectangles, 2½" × 4½"
4 squares, 2½" × 2½"

From the tan strips, cut a *total* of:
24 rectangles, 2½" × 4½"
4 squares, 2½" × 2½"

From the peach strips, cut a *total* of:
8 rectangles, 2½" × 4½"
4 squares, 2½" × 2½"

From the remaining assorted strips, cut a *total* of:
128 rectangles, 2½" × 4½"

From the coral print, cut:
6 strips, 1½" × 42"

From the navy print for middle border, cut:
7 strips, 1½" × 42"

From the navy dot, cut:
8 strips, 2½" × 42"

ASSEMBLING THE QUILT TOP

The quilt-top center is assembled in quadrants. Directions are for making one quadrant. Repeat to make a total of four quadrants. Press seam allowances in the directions indicated by the arrows.

1 Sort the pieces into the following groups. Make four of each group.

- **Gold:** 18 rectangles and 2 squares
- **Navy:** 13 rectangles and 2 squares
- **Cream:** 13 rectangles and 3 squares
- **Blue:** 15 rectangles and 2 squares
- **Slate:** 15 rectangles and 2 squares
- **Orange:** Nine rectangles and 1 square
- **Tan:** Six rectangles and 1 square
- **Peach:** Two rectangles and 1 square

2 For round 1, sew a gold square to a navy square. Sew a gold rectangle to the bottom of the two-square unit. Sew a navy rectangle to the right edge of the unit. The unit should measure 4½" × 6½", including seam allowances.

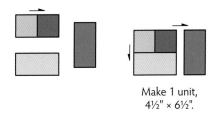

Make 1 unit,
4½" × 6½".

3 For round 2, sew a blue square to the end of a gold rectangle. Sew the unit to the bottom of the unit from step 2. Sew a cream square to the end of a navy rectangle; sew the unit to the right edge. The unit should measure 6½" × 8½", including seam allowances.

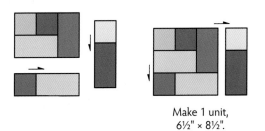

Make 1 unit,
6½" × 8½".

4 For round 3, sew a blue rectangle to the end of a gold rectangle. Sew the strip to the bottom of the unit from step 3. Sew a navy rectangle to the end of a cream rectangle. Sew the strip to the right edge. The unit should measure 8½" × 10½", including seam allowances.

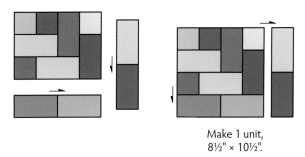

Make 1 unit,
8½" × 10½".

5 Referring to the following list, sew the pieces into strips. For each round, sew the first pieced strip to the bottom of the unit and the second pieced strip to the right edge of the unit.

Round 4: Join an orange square and blue and gold rectangles. Join a slate square and cream and navy rectangles.

Round 5: Join orange, blue, and gold rectangles. Join slate, cream, and navy rectangles.

Round 6: Join a slate square and orange, blue, and gold rectangles. Join a tan square and slate, cream, and navy rectangles.

Round 7: Join slate, orange, blue, and gold rectangles. Join tan, slate, cream, and navy rectangles.

Round 8: Join a gold square and slate, orange, blue, and gold rectangles. Join a blue square and tan, slate, cream, and navy rectangles.

Round 9: Join a slate, an orange, a blue, and two gold rectangles. Join blue, tan, slate, cream, and navy rectangles.

Round 10: Join a cream square and a slate, an orange, a blue, and two gold rectangles. Join a peach square and blue, tan, slate, cream, and navy rectangles.

Round 11: Join a cream, a slate, an orange, a blue, and two gold rectangles. Join peach, blue, tan, slate, cream, and navy rectangles.

Round 12: Join a navy square and a cream, a slate, an orange, a blue, and two gold rectangles. Join a cream square and peach, blue, tan, slate, cream, and navy rectangles.

Round 13: Join a navy, a cream, a slate, an orange, a blue, and two gold rectangles.

Sew the strips to the bottom and then right edges of the unit from step 4 to complete a quadrant that measures 28½" square, including seam allowances. Press all seam allowances away from the first square or rectangle. Repeat to make four quadrants.

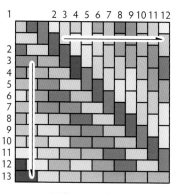

Make 4 quadrants, 28½" × 28½".

6 Lay out the quadrants in two rows of two, rotating the quadrants as shown. Sew the quadrants into rows. Join the rows to make the quilt-top center. The quilt center should measure 56½" square, including seam allowances.

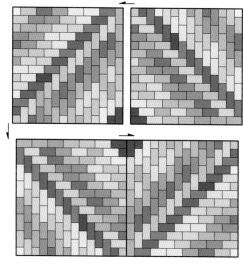

Quilt assembly

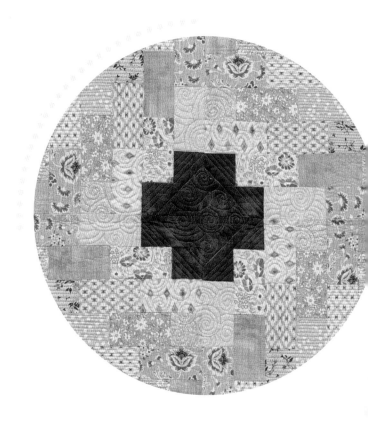

ADDING THE BORDERS

1 Join the coral strips end to end. From the pieced strip, cut two 58½"-long strips and two 56½"-long strips. Sew the 56½"-long strips to the top and bottom edges of the quilt center. Sew the 58½"-long strips to opposite sides of the quilt top. The quilt top should measure 58½" square, including seam allowances.

2 Join the navy print strips end to end. From the pieced strip, cut two 60½"-long strips and two 58½"-long strips. Sew the 58½"-long strips to the top and bottom edges of the quilt center. Sew the 60½"-long strips to opposite sides of the quilt top. The quilt top should measure 60½" square, including seam allowances.

3 Join 30 assorted rectangles to make a side border measuring 4½" × 60½", including seam allowances. Press the seam allowances open. Make two and sew them to opposite sides of the

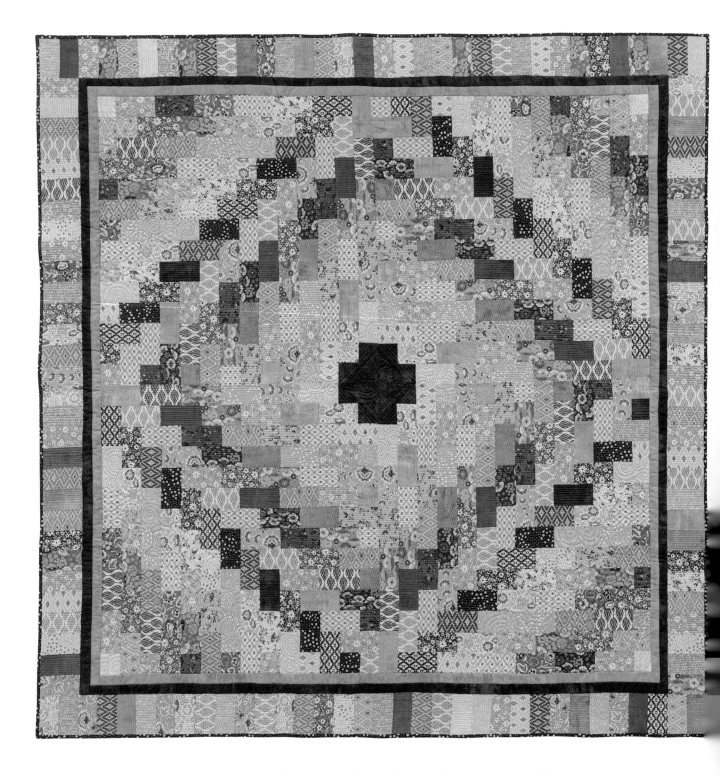

Designed and pieced by Lissa Alexander; quilted by Maggi Honeyman

quilt top. Join 34 assorted rectangles to make a top border measuring 4½" × 68½", including seam allowances. Press the seam allowances open. Repeat to make the bottom border. Sew these borders to the top and bottom edges. The quilt top should measure 68½" square.

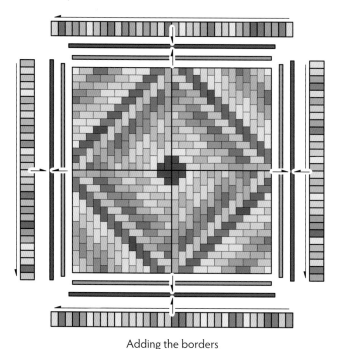

Adding the borders

FINISHING THE QUILT

For more details on any finishing steps, visit ShopMartingale.com/HowtoQuilt for free downloadable information.

1. Layer the quilt top with batting and backing; baste the layers together.

2. Quilt by hand or machine. Lissa's quilt is machine quilted with swirls in the navy center and across the light areas of the quilt. Back-and-forth lines are quilted in the darker rectangles in the quilt center and the outer border.

3. Use the navy dot 2½"-wide strips to make binding and then attach the binding to the quilt.

ROLLIN' WITH

Lissa Alexander

ModaLissa.com

I'd like to give a round of applause to quilters who press their seams open.

To start the ball rolling on a new project, I clean my machine, put in a new needle, pop a bag of popcorn and add M&M's, and I'm ready to go!

One phrase that rolls off the tongue easily at my house is "The kitchen is closed."

I'd gladly roll out the welcome mat for Keith Urban.

To round out my sewing basics of a ruler, mat, rotary cutter, and scissors, I'd add my steam iron and wool pressing mat.

I'd roll out the red carpet for the person who invented power car locks.

I roll into my sewing room around 7 p.m. on weeknights and early Saturday mornings.

When I let the good times roll, I'm sure to laugh until I snort.

I just roll with it when the dinner did not turn out quite like I planned.

My grandkids have me wrapped around their little fingers.

When I'm making the rounds at local quilt shops, I make sure to buy something at every stop.

In my home, we tend to gather 'round the kitchen counter.

Ask around and my friends will tell you I'm quirky, but patient.

Bird's-Eye View

Petite blocks line up with precision like a well-manicured garden seen from above. What's the secret to success? Try sewing with triangle paper foundations to deliver same-sized blocks again and again.

FINISHED QUILT: 59⅞" × 66⅛" | FINISHED BLOCK: 3⅛" × 3⅛"

MATERIALS

Yardage is based on 42"-wide fabric; Jelly Rolls contain 40 strips, 2½" × width of fabric. Lisa used American Gatherings by Primitive Gatherings.

- 1 Jelly Roll of assorted red and blue prints for blocks*
- 3⅝ yards of cream solid for setting squares, borders, and binding
- 3¾ yards of fabric for backing
- 66" × 73" piece of batting
- 1¼" finished Triangle Papers from Primitive Gatherings (optional)

You will need 12 red strips, 8 blue strips, 12 cream-with-red strips, and 8 cream-with-blue strips. The cream-with-red and cream-with-blue strips are referred to collectively as "light prints" throughout.

CUTTING

As you cut, keep like fabrics together. All measurements include ¼" seam allowances.

From *each* of 12 assorted red strips, cut:
2 strips, 1⅛" × 12" (24 total)
5 squares, 1⅛" × 1⅛" (60 total)

If using Triangle Papers, cut:
1 strip, 2½" × 24" (12 total)

If not using Triangle Papers, cut:
10 squares, 2⅛" × 2⅛" (120 total)

From *each* of 8 assorted blue strips, cut:
2 strips, 1⅛" × 12" (16 total)
5 squares, 1⅛" × 1⅛" (40 total)

If using Triangle Papers, cut:
1 strip, 2½" × 24" (8 total)

If not using Triangle Papers, cut:
10 squares, 2⅛" × 2⅛" (80 total)

From *each* of the 20 light strips, cut:
1 strip, 2½" × 12"; cut each strip into 2 pieces, 1⅛" × 12" (40 total)

If using Triangle Papers, cut:
1 strip, 2½" × 24" (20 total)

If not using Triangle Papers, cut:
10 squares, 2⅛" × 2⅛" (200 total)

From the cream solid, cut:
9 strips, 3⅝" × 42"; crosscut into 95 squares, 3⅝" × 3⅝"
10 strips, 6¾" × 42"; crosscut 4 of the strips into:
    2 strips, 6¾" × 28⅝"
    2 strips, 6¾" × 22⅜"
7 strips, 2½" × 42"

MAKING THE HALF-SQUARE-TRIANGLE UNITS

Pair each set of red or blue strips and squares with a set of light strips and squares from the same color family. You should have 12 sets of red strips and squares and 8 sets of blue strips and squares. Press seam allowances in the directions indicated by the arrows.

If Using Triangle Papers

1 Using a set of red and light 2½" × 24" strips, layer the strips right sides together with the light strip on top. Place a strip of triangle paper on top of the light print.

2 Shorten your stitch to half the normal length. Stitch on all the dashed lines. Cut apart on the solid lines using a rotary cutter and ruler.

3 With the paper still in place, press the seam allowances toward the red triangles. Remove the paper by pulling on it from the middle, near the seam. Clip the dog-ears to make 10 half-square-triangle units that measure 1¾" square, including seam allowances.

4 Repeat steps 1–3 using the remaining red, blue, and light 2½" × 24" strips to make 12 sets of 20 red (240 total) and 8 sets of 20 blue (160 total) half-square-triangle units. Eight red and eight blue units will be extra.

If Not Using Triangle Papers

1 Using a set of red and light 2⅛" squares, draw a diagonal line on the wrong side of the light squares.

2 Layer a marked square on a red square, right sides together. Sew ¼" from both sides of the drawn line. Cut the unit apart on the marked line to make two half-square-triangle units measuring 1¾" square, including seam allowances.

3 Repeat steps 1 and 2 to make 12 sets of 20 red units (240 total) and 8 sets of 20 blue units (160 total). Eight red units and eight blue units will be extra.

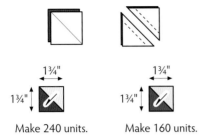

Make 240 units.   Make 160 units.

MAKING THE BLOCKS

1 Using a set of red and light 1⅛" × 12" strips, sew a red strip to the long edge of a light strip to make a strip set measuring 1¾" × 12", including seam allowances. Make two matching strip sets. Cut the strip sets into 20 segments, 1⅛" × 1¾".

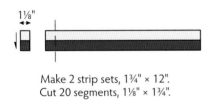

Make 2 strip sets, 1¾" × 12".
Cut 20 segments, 1⅛" × 1¾".

2 Repeat step 1 to make a total of 12 sets of 20 red segments and 8 sets of 20 blue segments.

3 Lay out four matching red half-square-triangle units, four matching red segments, and one red 1⅛" square in three rows of three. The red and light prints should be the same in all the pieces. Sew the pieces into rows. Join the rows to make a block. Make 58 red blocks measuring 3⅝" square, including seam allowances. You'll have eight segments and two squares left over for another project.

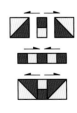

Make 58 blocks,
3⅝" × 3⅝".

4 Lay out four matching blue half-square-triangle units, four matching blue segments, and one blue 1⅛" square in three rows of three. The blue and light prints should be the same in all the pieces. Sew the pieces into rows. Join the rows to make a block. Make 38 blue blocks measuring 3⅝" square, including seam allowances. You'll have eight segments and two squares left over for another project.

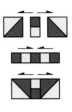

Make 38 blocks,
3⅝" × 3⅝".

Starch Your Way to Success

The absolute best way I've found to work precisely with small patchwork pieces is to starch all the fabrics before cutting and sewing. They will feel stiff when you sew them (that's what helps you be accurate!), but the quilt will soften as you handle it or wash it.

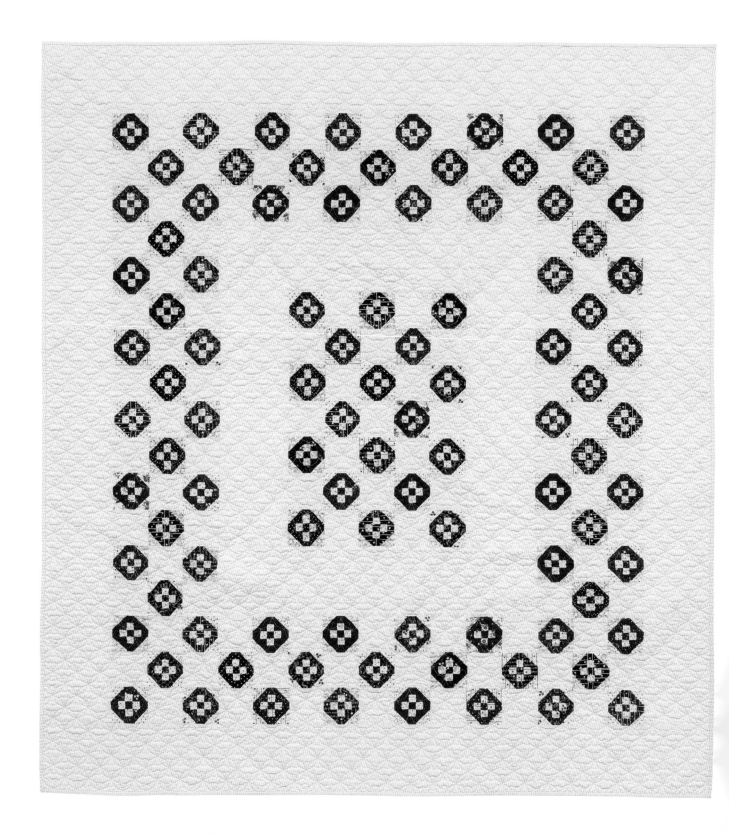

Designed and pieced by Lisa Bongean; quilted by Luke Neubauer

ASSEMBLING THE QUILT CENTER

Lay out 12 blue blocks, six red blocks, and 17 cream squares in seven rows of five, alternating the blocks and squares in each row and from row to row. Sew the blocks and squares into rows. Join the rows to make the quilt-top center. The quilt top should measure 16⅛" × 22⅜", including seam allowances.

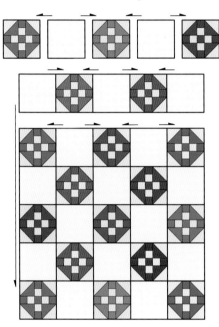

Quilt center unit,
16⅛" × 22⅜".

MAKING THE PIECED BORDERS

1 Join two red blocks and one cream 3⅝" square to make a border unit. Make 26 red border units measuring 3⅝" × 9⅞", including seam allowances.

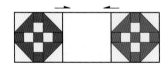

Make 26 units,
3⅝" × 9⅞".

2 Join two cream 3⅝" squares and one blue block to make a border unit. Make 26 blue border units measuring 3⅝" × 9⅞", including seam allowances.

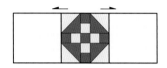

Make 26 units,
3⅝" × 9⅞".

3 Join six blue and five red units to make a side border. Make two borders measuring 9⅞" × 34⅞", including seam allowances. Join eight red and seven blue units to make a top border measuring 9⅞" × 47⅜", including seam allowances. Repeat to make the bottom border.

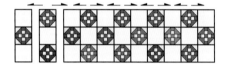

Make 2 side borders,
9⅞" × 34⅞".

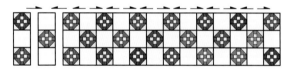

Make 2 top/bottom borders,
9⅞" × 47⅜".

ADDING THE BORDERS

1 Sew the cream 22⅜"-long strips to opposite sides of the quilt top. Sew the cream 28⅝"-long strips to the top and bottom edges. The quilt top should measure 28⅝" × 34⅞", including seam allowances.

2 Sew the shorter pieced borders to opposite sides of the quilt top. Sew the longer pieced borders to the top and bottom edges. The quilt top should measure 47⅜" × 53⅝", including seam allowances.

Lisa Bongean

LisaBongean.com

I'd like to give a round of applause to quilters who keep coming up with creative ideas to keep quilting alive and well.

To start the ball rolling on a new project, I go through my inspiration binders or admire my antique quilts.

One phrase that rolls off the tongue easily at my house is "I'm almost done."

I'd gladly roll out the welcome mat for quilters to gather and stitch together.

To round out my sewing basics of a ruler, mat, rotary cutter, and scissors, I'd add starch, of course!

I'd roll out the red carpet for the person who invented the rotary cutter. Who *did* invent the rotary cutter? We should know this!

When I let the good times roll, I'm sure to have a few little guys involved! (That's what I call my grandsons.) ☺

I just roll with it when things happen that I have no control over.

My grandsons have me wrapped around their little fingers.

When I'm making the rounds at local quilt shops, I make sure to buy something at each one and talk to the owners and sales clerks, telling them something I like about their shop.

In my home, we tend to gather 'round (on) the dock.

Ask around and my friends will tell you I'm up for an adventure. I've been called a daredevil a time or twenty!

③ Join the remaining cream 6¾"-wide strips end to end. From the pieced strip, cut two 53⅝"-long strips and two 59⅞"-long strips. Sew the shorter strips to opposite sides of the quilt center. Sew the longer strips to the top and bottom edges to complete the quilt top. The quilt top should measure 59⅞" × 66⅛".

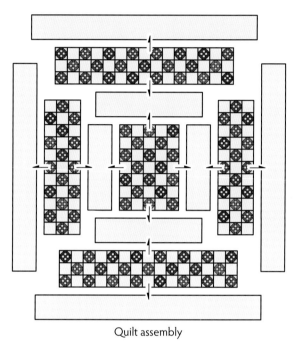

Quilt assembly

FINISHING THE QUILT

For more details on any finishing steps, visit ShopMartingale.com/HowtoQuilt for free downloadable information.

① Layer the quilt top with batting and backing; baste the layers together.

② Quilt by hand or machine. Lisa's quilt is machine quilted with an allover diamond and star design.

③ Use the cream 2½"-wide strips to make binding and then attach the binding to the quilt.

Circus

*This big top is delivering a ton of fun in no time at all! The main attraction?
Strip sets are cut into segments that make piecing blocks a breeze.
That's just the ticket for an easy-to-piece-and-complete quilt.*

FINISHED QUILT: 52½" × 52½" | FINISHED BLOCK: 16" × 16"

MATERIALS

*Yardage is based on 42"-wide fabric; Jelly Rolls contain
40 strips, 2½" × width of fabric. Barbara and Mary used
Back Porch by Me and My Sister Designs.*

- 1 Jelly Roll of assorted cream, blue, and red prints
  for blocks
- ½ yard of cream print for border
- ½ yard of blue print for binding
- 3⅜ yards of fabric for backing
- 59" × 59" piece of batting

CUTTING

*Divide the Jelly Roll strips into 18 pairs of 2 contrasting
or light and dark strips. As you cut the pieces, keep all
the pieces from each pair together. All measurements
include ¼" seam allowances.*

From *each* of 36 assorted print strips, cut:
1 strip, 2½" × 28" (36 total)
1 rectangle, 2½" × 8½" (36 total)

From the cream print for border, cut:
6 strips, 2½" × 42"

From the blue print, cut:
6 strips, 2½" × 42"

MAKING THE BLOCKS

Press seam allowances in the directions indicated by the arrows.

1 Using the strips from one set, join the 2½" × 28" strips to make a strip set measuring 4½" × 28", including seam allowances. Make a total of 18 strip sets. Cut each strip set into two 2½" × 4½" segments, two 4½" × 4½" segments, and two 4½" × 6½" segments.

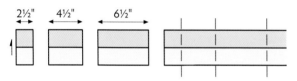

Make 18 strip sets, 4½" × 28".
Cut 2 segments, 2½" × 4½", 2 segments, 4½" × 4½",
and 2 segments, 4½" × 6½".

2 Using the segments from one strip set, lay out one 2½" × 4½" segment, one 4½" × 4½" segment, one 4½" × 6½" segment, and one matching 2½" × 8½" rectangle, noting the orientation of the segments. Join the segments, and then add the rectangle to the left edge. The quarter-block unit should measure 8½" square, including seam allowances.

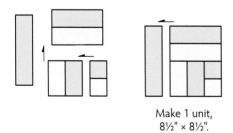

Make 1 unit,
8½" × 8½".

3 Lay out the remaining segments from the same strip set and the matching 2½" × 8½" rectangle, reversing the orientation of the segments. Join the segments, and then add the rectangle to the left edge. The quarter-block unit should measure 8½" square, including seam allowances.

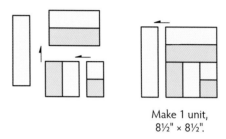

Make 1 unit,
8½" × 8½".

4 Repeat steps 2 and 3 to make a total of 36 quarter-block units.

5 Lay out four assorted quarter-block units in two rows of two. Sew the units into rows. Join the rows to make a block. Make nine blocks measuring 16½" square, including seam allowances.

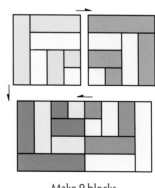

Make 9 blocks,
16½" × 16½".

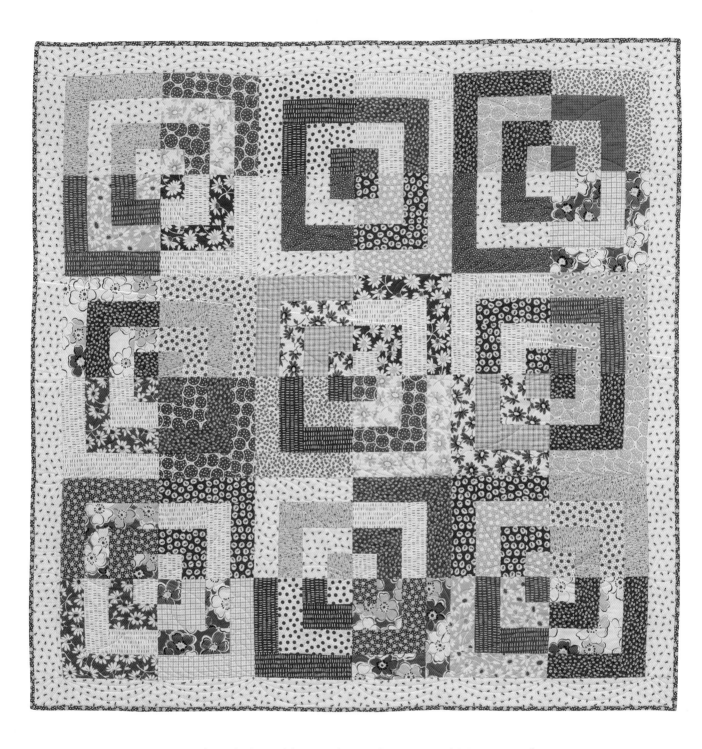

Designed and pieced by Barbara Groves and Mary Jacobson;
quilted by Sharon Elsberry

ASSEMBLING THE QUILT TOP

1 Lay out the blocks in three rows of three blocks each. Sew the blocks into rows and then join the rows. The quilt-top center should measure 48½" square, including seam allowances.

2 Join the cream 2½"-wide strips end to end. From the pieced strip, cut two 52½"-long strips and two 48½"-long strips. Sew the shorter strips to opposite sides of the quilt top. Sew the longer strips to the top and bottom edges. The quilt top should measure 52½" square.

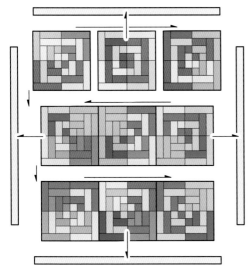

Quilt assembly

FINISHING THE QUILT

For more details on any finishing steps, visit ShopMartingale.com/HowtoQuilt for free downloadable information.

1 Layer the quilt top with batting and backing; baste the layers together.

2 Quilt by hand or machine. Barbara and Mary's quilt is machine quilted with an overlapping leaf motif in the center of the blocks. Feathers are quilted around the outer edges of the blocks and a swag motif is stitched in the border.

3 Use the blue 2½"-wide strips to make binding and then attach the binding to the quilt.

ROLLIN' WITH

Barbara Groves

MeandMySisterDesigns.com

I'd like to give a round of applause to quilters who love to sew and have learned to enjoy the process without perfection.

To start the ball rolling on a new project, I clean my cutting table, fill lots of bobbins, and empty the trash.

One phrase that rolls off the tongue easily at my house is "I'm sewing today, so you're on your own for dinner."

I'd gladly roll out the welcome mat for the UPS guy! He always seems to bring something I like.

To round out my sewing basics of a ruler, mat, rotary cutter, and scissors, I'd add pajama pants!

I'd roll out the red carpet for the person who invented the rotary cutter.

I roll into my sewing room around boxes. There is always a stack of boxes with fabric in them somewhere in my house.

When I let the good times roll, I'm sure to have family around.

I just roll with it when I have to get out the seam ripper. I might grumble, but I still roll!

My rescue dog Lucy has me wrapped around her little paw.

When I'm making the rounds at local quilt shops, I make sure to purchase something and look for yummy plaids.

Ask around and my friends will tell you I'm crazy in love with dogs!

Meet the Moda All-Stars

Susan Ache

Janet Clare

Lynne Hagmeier

Corey Yoder

Anne Sutton

Joanna Figueroa

Sherri McConnell

Vanessa Goertzen

Vanessa Christenson

Sandy Klop

April Rosenthal

Lissa Alexander

Lisa Bongean

Mary Jacobson

Barbara Groves

What's your creative passion?

Find it at **ShopMartingale.com**

books • eBooks • ePatterns • blog • free projects
videos • tutorials • inspiration • giveaways

Martingale®
Create with Confidence